50 MORE ROUTES

on

Scottish Mountains

RALPH STORER

David & Charles

To my mother and father
who also loved the mountains

A DAVID & CHARLES BOOK

First published 1987 as 100 Best Routes on Scottish Mountains
Reprinted 1988, 1989, 1991
This edition 1995
Paperback edition 1998

A catalogue record for this book is available from the British Library.

ISBN 0 7153 0698 7

Designed and edited by Cooling Brown, Hampton, Middlesex
Printed in Italy by Milanostampa SpA
for David & Charles
Brunel House, Newton Abbot, Devon

THE AUTHOR

Ralph Storer is an experienced and respected climber, walker and mountain biker who has pursued his chosen sports at the highest level. Currently a lecturer in computer studies at Napier University, Edinburgh, one of his great passions is for outdoor activities and the Scottish countryside. He writes regularly for mountaineering and walking magazines and is also the author of *50 Best Routes on Scottish Mountains, 50 Classic Routes on Scottish Mountains, 50 Best Routes on Skye and Raasay* and *Exploring Scottish Hill Tracks*, also published by David & Charles.

ACKNOWLEDGEMENTS

A book of this nature could not have been written without many years of experience on Scottish mountains or without the companionship of those who have accompanied me on the hill during these years. It would take too long and perhaps be inappropriate to thank all the companions who have climbed with me and aided, wittingly or unwittingly, in the writing of this book, for climbing forges bonds that need never be stated and can never be broken. I am grateful to all of them for the many hours spent in their company.

There are others without whose specific help this book could not have reached fruition. Donald MacDonald's advice on Gaelic was invaluable, although the phonetic interpretation of Gaelic pronunciation is my sole responsibility. Don Sargeant provided the sketch maps and Jo Crompton and Wendy Gibson provided transport and support during sometimes hectic days on the hill. I thank them all.

■ All photographs by the author except route 23 (Tom Rix) and route 25 (Mike Dixon). Cover photographs: (*front*) On the north ridge of Goat Fell; (*back*) On the north-west ridge of Beinn Tarsuinn (author)

CONTENTS

PREFACE TO THE SECOND EDITION

The second, all-colour, two-volume edition of *100 Best Routes on Scottish Mountains* follows seven years on from the first edition and incorporates a number of changes. Path changes over the years have affected Ben Venue (route 1), Cruach Ardrain (route 3), Mullach nan Coirean (route 11), the Aonachs (route 12), Streap (route 18), Beinn Dearg (route 36) and West Glen Rosa (route 43). Access problems have affected the approaches to Geal Charn (route 14), Sgurr Choinnich (route 24), Bidean a' Choire Sheasgaich (route 25) and the Fannichs (route 34). Two routes (A' Mhaighdean, route 32 and the Paps of Jura, route 46) have been reduced in length to make them more manageable. The new format has also enabled more detailed route descriptions to be given in many cases, and in a few cases route grids have been updated to reflect changes on the ground over the years. Many thanks to all readers who have written with suggestions.

The division of the 100 routes into two volumes of 50 has been done mainly on a geographical basis, to provide a cross-section of Highland hillwalking in each volume; the Islands section only has been divided on the basis of access, all Skye routes appearing in volume one (*50 Best Routes*) and all other island routes in volume two (*50 More Routes*).

I hope the routes presented in this book provide the reader with as much joy as they have the author.

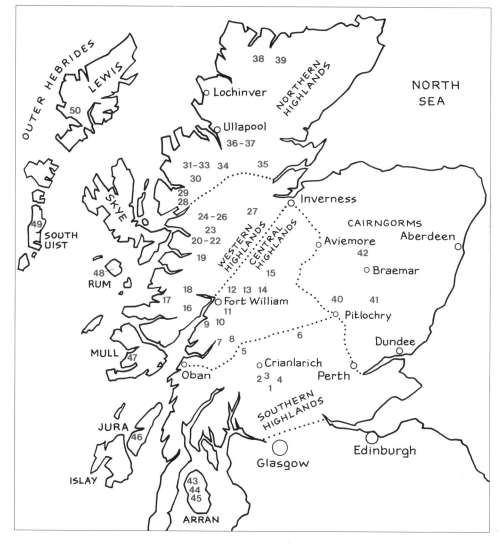

INTRODUCTION

The mountain walker in Scotland is spoilt for choice. In the Highlands there are 284 Munros (separate mountains over 3,000ft/914m), a further 227 Tops over 3,000ft/914m, 221 Corbetts (separate mountains over 2,500ft/762m) and countless lesser heights – enough to last a lifetime and more. The volumes in the *Best Routes* series contain a personal choice of the best walking and scrambling routes in this mountain playground, from short afternoon rambles to day-long expeditions, from roadside summits to remote mountain sanctuaries, from gentle paths to kneebreakingly-steep hillsides, from hands-in-pockets-whistle-while-you-walk strolls to thrilling scrambles.

Any book of this nature begs the question 'What constitutes *best*?', for beauty lies in the eye of the beholder. Some walkers may prefer the vast windswept plateaus of the Cairngorms in winter, others the sharp peaks of Skye on a long summer gloaming. The routes chosen are those I have found to be most enjoyable, would most want to repeat and would most recommend, given the following constraints:

1 A route must ascend a mountain over 2,000ft/610m. The fascination with Munros has for too long led to the neglect of some superb smaller mountains; of the 50 routes in this volume, 14 are on mountains under 3,000ft/914m.

2 A route must contain no rock climbing (ie on which a rope would normally be required).

This does not exclude some scrambles on which walkers of a nervous disposition would never venture – even with a safety net.

3 A route must start from a place that can be reached by motorised transport (plus a ferry if necessary), and end at the same place. There are too many guidebooks whose routes begin in the middle of nowhere and end somewhere else in the middle of nowhere.

4 A route must be able to be completed by walkers of reasonable fitness in a single day. This does not exclude some routes whose completion may be impracticable in daylight in the winter.

5 The overall list of routes must represent a cross-section of all the Highland regions. Fifty routes in the islands, no matter how attractive, would be unsuitable for a guidebook to the best of Scotland.

The list of suggested routes has already provoked many hours of heated debate among colleagues – yet the amount of agreement is surprising, so much so that I would venture to say that most experienced Scottish walkers would agree with the vast majority of mountains chosen (if not the exact routes). I hope that the following pages will help while away many a pleasant hour in planning, anticipation and reflection.

ROUTES
The 50 routes in this book are divided into six regions in accordance with accepted geographical divisions and common usage:
- The Southern Highlands: 6 routes – Routes 1-6
- The Central Highlands: 9 routes – Routes 7-15
- The Western Highlands: 12 routes – Routes 16-27
- The Northern Highlands: 12 routes – Routes 28-39
- The Cairngorms: 3 routes – Routes 40-42
- The Islands: 8 routes – Routes 43-50

Within each region routes are listed in approximately south-to-north, west-to-east order.

SKETCH MAPS
Sketch maps show each route's major features but are not intended for use on the hill. Ordnance Survey 1:50,000 scale maps are the most suitable for most Scottish mountain walking, but the OS 1:25,000 Outdoor Leisure maps to the Cuillin and Torridon Hills and the High Tops of the Cairngorms are recommended for these more complex areas. Beside each sketch map is indicated the number of the OS 1:50,000 map on which the route appears and the grid reference of the route's starting point (eg route 47 – OS: 48, GR: 507368). Some routes overlap two OS maps (eg route 30 – OS: 19/25) and others may appear on either of two maps (eg route 15 – OS: 34 or 42).

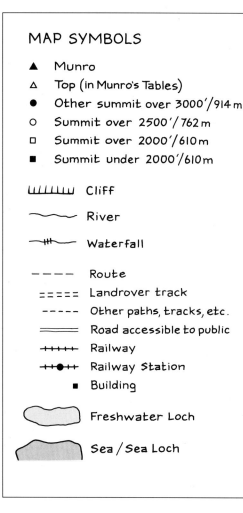

MAP SYMBOLS

▲ Munro
△ Top (in Munro's Tables)
● Other summit over 3000'/914 m
○ Summit over 2500'/762 m
□ Summit over 2000'/610 m
■ Summit under 2000'/610 m

ⓊⓊⓊⓊⓊⓊ Cliff

River

Waterfall

- - - - - Route
===== Landrover track
- - - - - Other paths, tracks, etc.
Road accessible to public
+++++ Railway
++●++ Railway Station
■ Building

Freshwater Loch

Sea / Sea Loch

The classification of mountains as Munros or Tops is based on the 1997 edition of *Munro's Tables*, incorporating revisions made since the 1891 publication of Sir Hugh Munro's original list, which contained 283 Munros and a further 255 Tops. Many walkers (including the author) regret any tampering with Sir Hugh's list, apart from reclassification following revision of heights on the map, but the latest edition is the *de facto* arbiter of the Tables. There are no clear criteria of what makes a mountain a Munro, a Top or neither, beyond the definition of a Munro as a separate mountain over 3,000ft/914m and a Top as a subsidiary summit over 3,000ft/914m.

MEASUREMENTS

Route distances are specified in both miles (to the nearest half-mile) and kilometres (to the nearest kilometre); short distances in the text are specified in metres (an approximate imperial measurement is yards).

Mountain heights are specified in metres and feet. Metric heights have been obtained from OS 2nd Series 1:50,000 maps. Equivalent heights in feet have been obtained by multiplying the height in metres by 3.28 (rounded down); these may not tally with heights on old OS one-inch-to-the-mile maps, which were obtained from an earlier survey.

The total amount of ascent for the whole route is specified to the nearest 10m (50ft). This is an approximation based on OS map heights and contours, which are shown at 10m intervals and are in many instances omitted because of cartographic complexity.

Route times (to the nearest half-hour) are based on the time it should take a person of reasonable fitness to complete the route in good summer conditions. They take into account length of route, amount of ascent, technical difficulty, type of terrain and short stoppages, but do not make allowances for long stoppages and adverse weather. They are roughly standard between routes for comparison purposes, and can be adjusted where necessary by a factor appropriate to the individual.

In winter, routes will normally take much longer, depending on conditions. A pre-dawn start is often necessary and some of the longer routes are best tackled as two-day expeditions, camping en route or making use of a bothy (useful bothies are noted in the text).

MOUNTAIN NAMES

Most Highland names are Gaelic in origin and the ability to pronounce and understand Gaelic names can add much to the pleasure of walking in Scotland. To this end a guide to the meaning of all mountain names is given in the Glossary/Index *(p110)* and a guide to pronunciation is given below.

The production of such a guide is made difficult by a number of factors. OS maps, despite their otherwise excellence, appear to have been named by Sassenachs, for they abound in Gaelic misspellings, misunderstandings, misuses and misplacements. It is with some misgivings that the author has retained OS spellings for the purpose of standardisation, except in the case of Rum, whose OS 'h' (Rhum) was added out of Victorian prudishness and should no longer be tolerated. Some OS misspellings make pronounciation impossible. In addition, some names have become anglicised to such an extent that it would be pedantic to enforce a purist pronunciation on a non-Gaelic speaker. For example, the correct pronunciation of Ben is something akin to Pane, with a soft *n* as in the first syllable of *onion*. Moreover, pronunciation differs, sometimes markedly, throughout the Highlands and Islands.

Despite these problems, the phonetic guide given below and shown in the Glossary should enable a good attempt at a pronunciation that would be intelligible to a Gaelic speaker:

Y before a vowel pronounced as in *you*
OW pronounced as in *town*
CH pronounced as in Scottish *loch* or
   German *noch*
TCH pronounced as *ch* in *church*
Œ pronounced as in French *oeuf* or the
   u in *turn*

Toponomy (the study of place name meanings) is complicated by OS misspellings, changes in spelling and in word usage over the centuries, as well as by words with more than one meaning and unknown origin of names (Gaelic, Norse, Irish etc). For example, consider the origin of the name Rois-Bheinn (see route 17). Meanings given in this book are the most commonly accepted, even if disputed; when the meaning is doubtful it is annotated with poss (ie possible); some names are too obscure to be given any meaning.

ASSESSMENT AND SEASONAL NOTES

The Assessment is intended as a brief overview of the nature of the route during summer conditions. Under snow, Scottish mountains become much more serious propositions. Paths are totally obliterated, grassy hillsides become treacherous slopes, ridges become corniced, stone shoots become snow gullies, walking becomes far more difficult and tiring, the contoured terrain becomes featureless in adverse weather, and white-outs and spindrift reduce visibility to zero.

Winter conditions vary from British to Alpine to Arctic from November through to April, though sometimes earlier and later and varying from locality to locality – it is possible to encounter hard snow and ice even in October and May.

It cannot be stressed enough that no-one should venture into the Scottish mountains in winter without adequate clothing, an ice-axe and experience (or the company of an experienced person). In hard winter conditions crampons will also be required.

The number of accidents – many of them fatal – which have occurred in Scotland over the last few winters should leave no-one in doubt as to the need for caution.

Many of the routes in this book become major mountaineering expeditions in winter and should not be attempted by walkers; such routes are indicated in Seasonal Notes. The viability of other routes in winter depends on grade and conditions; in general the higher the summer grade, the higher the winter grade. Note, however, that even a normally straight-forward winter route may be subject to avalanche or hard ice, to say nothing of potentially life-threatening, severe winter weather.

The Scottish mountains in winter have an Alpine attraction and reward the prepared walker with unforgettable experiences, but if - in doubt, stay off the hill. Bearing these points in mind, the Seasonal Notes for each route indicate any specific places where particular difficulties are normally likely to be encountered, thus enabling the walker to be better prepared. Where an easier escape route presents itself this also is noted.

ROUTE DIFFICULTY

The overall difficulty of each route is shown in the form of a grid, as explained on page 9. It will be apparent from this grading system that not all the routes in this book are for novices. Many accidents in the Scottish hills are caused by walkers attempting routes outside their capabilities, and the grading system is intended to enable a more realistic route appraisal. On the more technically difficult routes, easier alternatives are noted in the text or else in the seasonal notes, if applicable.

ACCESS

Any access restrictions on the routes are noted in the text, apart from stalking restrictions. Whatever one's ethical stance on deer stalking, the fact remains that most of the Scottish Highlands is privately owned, and non-compliance with stalking restrictions is likely to be counter-productive and may well lead to the imposition of further restrictions. In addition, if estate revenue is lost because of interference with stalking activities, the alternative may be afforestation or worse – which would not only increase access problems but could irreparably alter the landscape.

The stalking season for stags runs normally from mid-August to mid-October, but varies from locality to locality. Access notices dot the roadside and information on stalking activities can be obtained from estate offices and head stalkers. For a complete list of access restrictions and estate addresses see *Access for Mountaineers and Hillwalkers*, which is published jointly by the Mountaineering Council of Scotland and the Scottish Landowners' Federation.

Land shown on the OS map as belonging to public bodies, such as the National Trust for Scotland and Scottish Natural Heritage, is normally not subject to access restrictions.

Finally, it should be noted that all river directions given in the text as 'left bank' and 'right bank', in accordance with common usage, refer to the direction you will be pointing towards when facing downstream.

GRID

	1	2	3	4	5
grade					
terrain					
navigation					
seriousness					

An at-a-glance grid for each route indicates the route's overall difficulty, where difficulty consists not only of **grade** (ie technical difficulty) but also type of **terrain** (irrespective of grade), difficulty of **navigation** with a compass in adverse weather, and **seriousness** (ie difficulty of escape in case of curtailment of route for one reason or another. This is based upon a criteria of length and restricted line of escape). These factors vary over the duration of the route and should not be taken as absolute, but they do provide a useful general guide and enable comparisons to be made between routes. Each category is graded, ranging from 1 (easiest) to 5 (hardest).

Grade
1 Mostly not too steep
2 Appreciable steep sections
3 Some handwork required
4 Easy scramble
5 Hard scramble

Terrain
1 Excellent, often on paths
2 Good
3 Reasonable
4 Rough
5 Tough

Navigation
1 Straightforward
2 Reasonably straightforward
3 Appreciable accuracy required
4 Hard
5 Extremely hard

Seriousness
1 Straightforward escape
2 Reasonably straightforward escape
3 Appreciable seriousness
4 Serious
5 Very serious

Investigating a spur ridge near the summit of Spidean Mialach (Route 19).

	1	2	3	4	5
grade					
terrain					
navigation					
seriousness					

OS MAP: 57
GR: 503064
DISTANCE: 5½ miles (9km)
ASCENT: 670m (2,200ft)
TIME: 4½ hours

ASSESSMENT: a short and pleasant route amidst rugged and picturesque scenery on the edge of the Highlands. Sections of new all-weather path ease the ascent as far as the edge of the forest, but upper Gleann Riabhach can become very boggy after rain. **NB** Continued forest road and path construction may affect the route; look for signposts.

SEASONAL NOTES: in winter the ascent normally remains easy and a good introduction to walking on snow, but care is required if descending the steeper north side on snow.

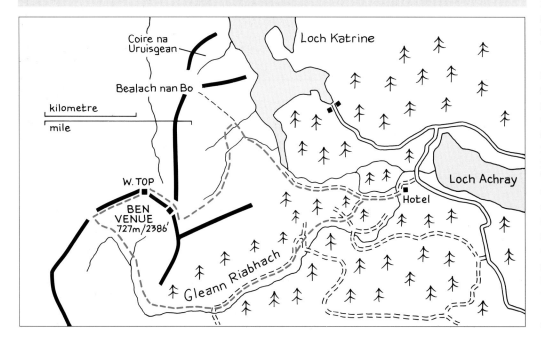

'High on the south, huge Benvenue
Down on the lake in masses threw
Crags, knolls and mounds, confusedly hurled,
The fragments of an earlier world.'

SIR WALTER SCOTT
(The Lady of the Lake, 1810)

Ben Venue is a modest but rugged mountain whose craggy, wooded slopes enclose the island-studded eastern reaches of Loch Katrine in the Trossachs and give the engaging impression of a miniature Highland scene. It was here that Sir Walter Scott, Coleridge and the Wordsworths, among others, found inspiration.

The view of Ben Venue across Loch Achray to the east is one of the most photographed in the Trossachs, and the most pleasant ascent is also from this side. Begin at Loch Achray Hotel on the west side of the loch. Behind the hotel a forest road leads off into the trees. After five minutes keep left at a fork and after another five minutes keep straight on at a crossroads. The road reaches the river that flows down Gleann Riabhach and a path continues straight on to join a higher forest road. Go left along this road for one hundred metres then branch right on a path that rejoins it higher up. Continue along the road until it does a U-turn across the river, then take the continuing path that climbs to the forest edge and out into upper Gleann Riabhach.

Once out of the trees the path turns right into the craggy upper glen, bypassing a water-

fall and climbing to a large cairn on Ben Venue's rugged south-west ridge. Turn right to gain the west top, a grand viewpoint from where the main peaks of the Southern Highlands can be picked out one by one across Loch Katrine. The higher east top of Ben Venue's twin summits is a short distance further along.

To descend, go down the wide grass gully just beyond the summit, making for the islands of Loch Katrine that nestle attractively beneath your feet. Lower down, the best going is to be found on the right of the main stream but, when the first trees are reached, it is important to keep well to the left, close under Ben Venue's north ridge, to avoid tree-girt crags above the lochside. A path on the left of the stream that is next left of the main stream eventually leads down to join the path that runs along the south shore of the loch to a forest road and your starting point.

The south shore path comes from the

Ben Venue from Loch Achray.

Bealach nam Bo (Pass of the Cattle), the rocky defile on Ben Venue's north ridge, whose name derives from Rob Roy's smuggling days. Just below the bealach, among the crags above the lochside, is the Coire na Uruisgean (Goblin's Cave), which may give the mountain its name (Mountain of the Cave), although more of a deep amphitheatre than a cave; some amusement may be had searching for it.

Route 2: THE GLEN FALLOCH GROUP • THE SOUTHERN HIGHLANDS

	1	2	3	4	5
grade					
terrain					
navigation					
seriousness					

OS MAP: 50 or 56
GR: 352219
DISTANCE: 10½ miles (17km)
ASCENT: 1,250m (4,100ft)
TIME: 8 hours

ASSESSMENT: a grassy ridge walk over complex terrain, passing a number of fascinating physical features, with considerable routefinding difficulties should the mist descend.

SEASONAL NOTES: a fine, if somewhat lengthy, winter's tramp. No technical difficulties are normally encountered, but competence on sometimes steep snow slopes is required.

The trio of Munros that form the Glen Falloch group were made mainly for those who like a good long tramp through the grass and heather, but to add spice to the route, some of the most interesting physical features in the Southern Highlands will also be found hidden on their long, complex ridges.

Begin at the private road to Derrydarroch Farm in Glen Falloch, 3 miles (5km) south-west of Crianlarich on the A82. Follow the road across the River Falloch (bridge), then make directly across the rough moor for the summit of Sron Gharbh at the end of Twistin Hill. Twistin Hill is the undulating grassy ridge that forms the attractive skyline ahead and provides the best approach to An Caisteal, the first of the three peaks. Near the summit of An Caisteal the ridge steepens and displays some curious features; on the left, a number of small caves burrow into the hillside and a large cleft almost cuts the ridge in two. Beyond lies the castellated knoll which probably gives the mountain its name (The Castle), and then easier slopes lead to the flat summit.

To continue to Beinn a' Chroin, the second Munro, descend An Caisteal's grassy south-east ridge on a path that winds down among outcrops to the bealach between the two mountains. From here, thread your way up Beinn a' Chroin's steep craggy west face to the west top, then follow the ½ mile (1km) long summit ridge eastwards across a dip to the higher east top. To continue to Beinn Chabhair, the third Munro, first return to the bealach before An

Derrydarroch

SRON GHARBH
708m/2322'

STOB GLAS

TWISTIN HILL

Glen Falloch

STOB CREAG AN FHITHICH
685m/2250'

Lochan a Chaisteil

AN CAISTEAL
995m/3264'

BEINN A' CHROIN
946m/3103'

A82

WEST HIGHLAND WAY

BEINN CHABHAIR
933m/3060'

kilometre

mile

Caisteal. From here, descend the grassy gully on the south side for about 50m (150ft), until a traverse right can be made below outcrops across the undulating hillside to the lochan at the foot of Beinn Chabhair's north-east ridge. A stiff 300m (1,000ft) pull on steep grass among outcrops is then required to gain the summit.

The north-west ridge that leads back down to Glen Falloch is the most interesting of the day. Quite narrow near the top, it soon broadens over some steep drops. Further down, the terrain is extraordinarily complex, and at times it seems difficult to make any progress through the labyrinth of grassy knolls. At the end of the ridge steer left of Stob Creag an Fhithich to reach the delightful secret hollow that cradles Lochan

Sron Gharbh (left) and An Caisteal (right) from Glen Falloch.

a' Chaisteil, whose surrounding crags fall straight into the water and give the fanciful appearance of a castle. From here, aim northwards to join the West Highland Way path along the River Falloch back to Derrydarroch.

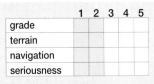

Route 3: CRUACH ARDRAIN • THE SOUTHERN HIGHLANDS

	1	2	3	4	5
grade					
terrain					
navigation					
seriousness					

OS MAP: 50/51/56
GR: 382245
DISTANCE: 7 miles (11km)
ASCENT: 1,010m (3,300ft)
TIME: 5½ hours

ASSESSMENT: an undulating skyline walk around an extensive corrie, which includes an interesting traverse of the highest peak.

SEASONAL NOTES: the descent from Cruach Ardrain towards Stob Garbh is steep and difficult in winter; it can be turned by a descent into the south-east corrie, but care is required in finding a line back to the bealach before Stob Garbh. The conspicuous Y-shaped gully that splits the north face of Cruach Ardrain makes a sporting winter climb.

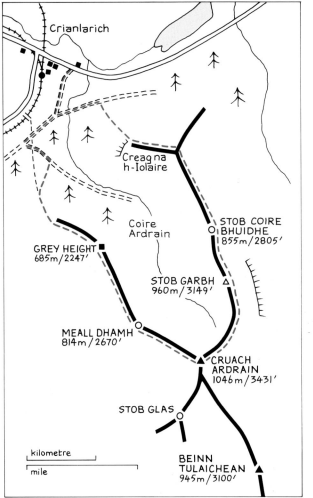

The Glen Falloch group (Route 2) and Ben More and Stob Binnein (Route 4 in *50 Best Routes*) form five of the seven Munros known as the Crianlarich Hills. Cruach Ardrain and Beinn Tulaichean are the remaining two mountains; like their neighbours, they are characterised by long twisting ridges that are mainly grassy but studded with rock outcrops, and they make good high tramping country. The fine wedge-shaped peak of Cruach Ardrain rises prominently above the forests of Coire Ardrain. Forestry operations cause access to be in a state of constant change but, once onto the open mountainside, the round of the undulating corrie skyline makes a very pleasant stravaig. From the summit, Beinn Tulaichean can be reached by an optional add-on.

Begin on the forest road that leaves the A85 immediately west of the Benmore Hotel on the eastern outskirts of Crianlarich. Keep right at the first junction and left at the second to cross a line of old fence posts that marks the route of the old path up Cruach Ardrain, now in an execrable state. Look for the clearing on the right a few hundred metres past the fence, at the far end of which the skyline comes into view for the first time. Leave the forest road here and climb the clearing to its end at a T-junction, then bear right to join the last boggy section of the old path and gratefully reach open ground on the north-west shoulder of the Grey Height, whose top is then easily gained.

A broad grassy ridge leads onwards to Meall Dhamh and then things become more interesting. The path negotiates a steep drop and descends 160ft (50m) before winding among rocky knolls and climbing steeply onto the flat roof of Cruach Ardrain (in mist note that the summit lies across a dip beyond the first two cairns reached). Beinn Tulaichean lies south-east of the summit and can be bagged by a return trip that will add 2½ miles (4km), 350m (1,150ft) and about 2 hours to the day. Continuing around Coire Ardrain, a steep rocky descent (requiring care) leads to a bealach and onto the rocky peak of Stob Garbh, beyond which there is a pleasant descent along the eastern arm of Coire Ardrain to Creag na h-Iolaire.

From here, descend steep grass slopes on the right to an obvious firebreak leading down into the trees. When the break ends at a transverse clearing, keep descending on a developing path, first tunnelling through the trees to another transverse clearing, then following a narrow break down to a forest road. Turn left to follow the road back to the first junction on the outward route and turn right here to reach your starting point.

Cruach Ardrain (centre) from near Crianlarich.

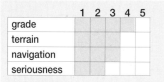

	1	2	3	4	5
grade				▣	
terrain			▣		
navigation		▣			
seriousness			▣		

OS MAP: 51/57
GR: 602224
DISTANCE: 9½ miles (15km)
ASCENT: 1,130m (3,700ft)
TIME: 7½ hours

ASSESSMENT: a circuit of two popular peaks that combines an easy ascent of the first with a more problematical ascent of the second. **NB** Although graded 4, there is a grade 2 alternative on steep ground.

SEASONAL NOTES: in winter, care should be exercised on the steep, convex summit slopes of Ben Vorlich, where a slip on the north side has caused at least one fatality. The ascent of Stuc a' Chroin is a much more serious winter proposition and is not for the inexperienced.

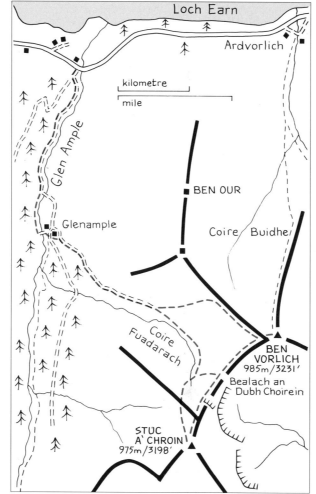

The south side of Loch Earn is dominated by the interesting X-shaped mountain of Ben Vorlich, and behind it lies its hidden neighbour Stuc a' Chroin, whose north-east prow towers over the Bealach an Dubh Choirein between the two mountains and whose ascent proves to be even more interesting. The most popular route up Ben Vorlich is the path from Ardvorlich, but the easiest approach to the round of both peaks is the Land Rover track that begins at the foot of Glen Ample on the South Loch Earn road, 1 mile (1½km) east of its junction with the A84.

Keep left after a hundred metres to follow the track along the west bank of the Burn of Ample. When the track crosses the river to Glenample Farm, keep to the path on the near bank and cross at the next bridge. Leave the main path and climb around the farm's perimeter fence, crossing one track to reach another, grassier one. This climbs through forestry plantations to end at a height of nearly 550m (1,800ft) on open hillside in Coire Fuadarach, from where the traverse of the two mountains amounts to a circuit of the corrie skyline.

From the end of the track make a rising traverse across the grassy hillside to the foot of Ben Vorlich's north-west ridge, then climb the steepening ridge to the summit. The summit is a 100 metres long ridge slung between two tops; the trig. pillar on the west top is one metre higher than the cairn on the east top. As befits a peak on the edge of the Highlands, the view is extensive but distant.

A well-worn path weaves its way down among outcrops to the Bealach an Dubh Choirein and then climbs to the foot of Stuc a' Chroin's prow. By weaving back and forth on the broken crags that form the crest, an easy and entertaining scramble can be had. The path veers right of the crest but also involves handwork, and it is now so worn and gritty, with some exposure and an increasing number of variations, that it cannot be recommended to anyone who is looking for an easy way up.

For a trouble-free ascent, leave the main path at the bealach for a developing path that descends slightly around the foot of outcrops and traverses into the shallow corrie right of the prow. From here the path climbs steeply up the back of the corrie to reach a shallow saddle on Stuc a' Chroin's north-west ridge. Once the prow has been climbed or circumvented, easy slopes continue to the summit.

The best way back down to Coire Fuadarach is to descend the path from the saddle, although this is also becoming worn and care is required on its steep upper section. In good visibility the saddle can be reached by a direct line from the summit, which avoids the awkward boulderfield formed where the upper part of the north-west ridge rises to meet the top of the prow. In mist it is better to go to the top of the prow (cairn) and then down the north-west ridge to the saddle; do not be misled by a cairn at the top of a stone shoot a short distance before reaching the saddle. Cross the floor of the corrie to regain the track back down to Glen Ample.

Making it look harder than it is on the prow of Stuc a' Chroin, with Ben Vorlich behind.

Route 5: BEINN DORAIN AND BEINN AN DOTHAIDH • THE SOUTHERN HIGHLANDS

	1	2	3	4	5
grade					
terrain					
navigation					
seriousness					

OS MAP: 50
GR: 300395
DISTANCE: 7½ miles (12km)
ASCENT: 1,270m (4,150ft)
TIME: 6 hours

ASSESSMENT: a straight-forward ascent, with fine corrie scenery and commanding views on the edge of Rannoch Moor.

SEASONAL NOTES: in winter the steep slopes leading up to the bealach require care under snow. Winter routefinding can be especially difficult in mist

(Beinn an Dothaidh's summit cornice demands particular attention).

MAP NOTE: the tri-topped summit plateau of Beinn an Dothaidh is incorrectly represented on OS maps prior to 1984.

*' 'Twas health and strength, 'twas life
and joy, to wander freely there,
To drink at the fresh mountain stream,
to breathe the mountain air.'*

*On Beinn Dorain by DUNCAN BAN
MACINTYRE, born Inveroran 1724.*

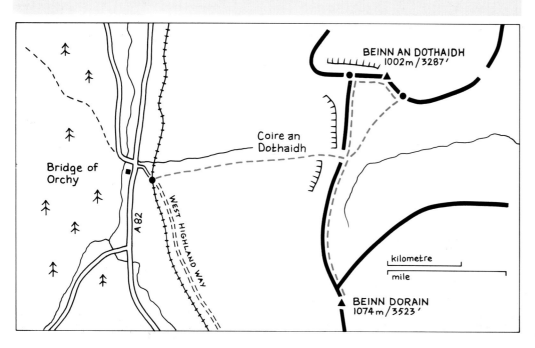

The huge pyramid of Beinn Dorain is a familiar landmark that dominates the landscape between Tyndrum and Bridge of Orchy and has inspired many a hillwalker, including the famous local Gaelic poet Duncan Ban MacIntyre. Its clean unbroken lines sweep up dramatically to a steep summit cone, forming one of the steepest grass slopes in the Highlands and dwarfing the West Highland Railway line that contours around its foot and gives scale to the scene. Yet the ascent of Beinn Dorain is not as difficult as it looks, for to the north it presents an easy-angled ridge that descends to a bealach, and the bealach itself is easily reached from a high corrie (Coire an Dothaidh) above Bridge of Orchy. The bealach also connects Beinn Dorain to Beinn an Dothaidh and enables the latter summit to be taken in on the same expedition, to give a panoramic view of Rannoch Moor that is worth any effort.

Begin at Bridge of Orchy railway station car park. Go through the underpass, cross a cart track that forms part of the West Highland Way and follow the somewhat boggy path that climbs the left bank (right side) of the burn into

the rough confines of Coire an Dothaidh. The path contours left around a steepening into the upper corrie and from there a short ascent leads to the bealach between the two mountains. Turn right to climb Ben Dorain's broad north ridge, which rises steadily before easing off to a false summit at the junction with the north-east ridge (a very confusing spot in mist). The true summit lies a short distance further along across a pleasantly narrow saddle. Views of the glen below seem almost aerial.

Retrace your steps to the bealach (surprisingly awkward in mist) and climb more steeply up the broad south ridge of Beinn an Dothaidh to a point that marks the edge of the stony summit plateau (another very confusing place in mist). Keep going to reach the west top at the cliff-edge of the impressive north-east corrie,

Approaching the summit of Ben Dorain.

then turn right to follow the corrie rim to the true summit, from where there is an unforgettable view over the huge triangle of flatness and desolation that is Rannoch Moor. Further right is a third and lower top that can be visited, and from there you can make a beeline back to the bealach and so to Bridge of Orchy.

Route 6: SCHIEHALLION • THE SOUTHERN HIGHLANDS

	1	2	3	4	5
grade					
terrain					
navigation					
seriousness					

OS MAP: 42 or 51
GR: 753557
DISTANCE: 6 miles (10km)
ASCENT: 760m (2,500ft)
TIME: 4½ hours

ASSESSMENT: a straight-forward route up the backbone of the Fairy Hill, but note that the path is eroded and can become very boggy after rain.

SEASONAL NOTES: a normally easy introduction to the possibilities of winter walking in Scotland. The only difficulty that may be encountered is where the route steepens to join the east ridge.

CAVING NOTE: unusually for the Southern Highlands, the northern flanks of Schiehallion contain a number of small limestone caves.

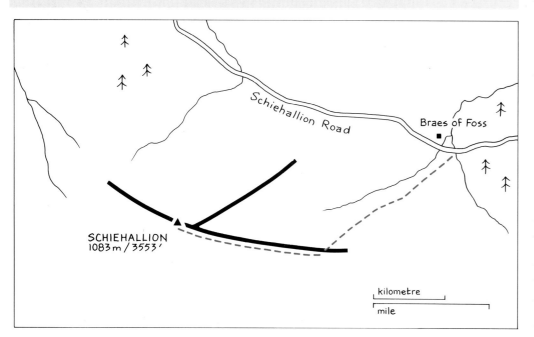

Situated centrally between east and west coasts and isolated by deep glens on all sides, Schiehallion (The Fairy Hill of the Caledonians) is a familiar landmark in many views. From the west, across Loch Rannoch or even from 30 miles (50km) away across Rannoch Moor, it shows up as a graceful symmetrical cone, which has a formidable appearance in white winter raiment, but its true character is revealed in eastern views such as that from the Queen's View across Loch Tummel, from where its long whaleback ridge can be seen sprawling over the moors. The evenly weathered quartzite that gives Schiehallion its regularity and makes it attractive and photogenic indicates a lack of variety for the walker, but this is compensated for by the mountain's splendid isolation, its niche in mountaineering history, the ease of its ascent and its extensive summit views.

The recommended route is the *voie normale* from Schiehallion Road (the minor road that crosses Schiehallion's northern flank to link the B846 with Kinloch Rannoch). The route has a path or cairns all the way and approaches the summit via the gentle east ridge, thus avoiding the mountain's steeper sides and saving the view westwards as reward for gaining the summit.

Begin at Braes of Foss car park, just east of the farm of that name, and take the well trodden path that goes around the edge of forestry plantations and across the heathery moor to climb onto the broad east ridge. The only navigational difficulty on the moor, worth

Schiehallion from the north.

noting for the return journey, is where the path zigzags across two forks of a track coming up from Braes of Foss farm. The wide, eroded path is often boggy as far as the ridge and is best avoided after rain.

Once onto the ridge, turn right and follow the cairned path as it climbs inexorably up the broad whaleback ridge, which becomes increasingly well-defined as peat gives way to broken and occasionally tiresome quartzite underfoot. As the path disappears on stony ground cairns mark the route onward, although in fine weather the way is obvious. There are enough false tops to last a lifetime and the ascent becomes psychologically rather than physically challenging. The ridge eventually eases and narrows pleasantly to an unexpectedly interesting craggy summit, where scramblers with withdrawal symptoms can even seek one or two moves to occupy their hands. This is an often exposed and windy spot, but it commands wonderful views to the north and west over a mosaic of loch and woodland scenery. On descent in cloud the broadening ridge can be very misleading and it is important not to lose the line of cairns among all the other piles of rock.

Historical note: in 1774 Nevil Maskelyne, the Astronomer Royal, was attracted to Schiehallion by its regularity of shape, which he was able to utilise in his experiments on the estimation of the mass of the earth.

During this project Charles Hutton, one of the survey team, had the idea of drawing lines on the map to connect points of equal height and thus contour lines were born.

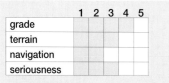

	1	2	3	4	5
grade					
terrain					
navigation					
seriousness					

OS MAP: 50
GR: 136468
DISTANCE: 8 miles (13km)
ASCENT: 1,100m (3,600ft)
TIME: 6½ hours

ASSESSMENT: a steep ascent gives access to exhilarating high-level ridge walking.

SEASONAL NOTES: a magnificent winter route for budding Alpinists. A rope is hardly required, although the upper section of the north ridge is usually quite exposed. The traverse to Stob Coire Dheirg can be avoided if necessary by a descent into the south-east corrie followed by a traverse beneath the crest.

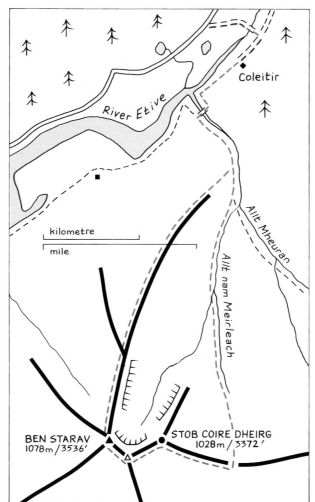

The bold peak of Ben Starav occupies a commanding position at the head of Loch Etive, which is reached by the road that leaves the A82 Glen Coe road at the western edge of Rannoch Moor and strikes south-west along long and beautiful Glen Etive. The mountain's striking symmetry and airy twin summits give it a classic appearance, but it is probably its massive stature, which becomes ever more imposing as you drive along the glen, that gives it its Gaelic name (Bold Mountain).

The obvious route of ascent is via the north ridge, which sweeps up steeply from the glen directly to the summit, the rightmost of the twin peaks. Right from the start the ridge can be seen in its entirety and, with its steepness enhanced by foreshortening, the effort required to ascend it will for once not be underestimated. The climb is relentless but straightforward; ever expanding views and increasingly rocky surroundings maintain interest, and there is always the promise of more exciting things to come.

Begin on the Glen Etive road at the track to Coleitir Cottage, 2½ miles (4km) from the road end. Take the track to the cottage and the path that continues beyond, keeping right at a fork about 100 metres beyond the cottage. The path reaches the Allt Mheuran and crosses it by a bridge 200 metres upstream, and then a path on the left bank (right side) continues up to a pine-studded gorge at the foot of the north ridge. Climb the ridge direct; it is steep and grassy at first, and the angle eases only twice,

once at about 500m (1,650ft) and again at about 850m (2,800ft) when another ridge joins from the right. Above this latter levelling the final 200m (650ft) section to the summit steepens again and becomes narrower and more boulder-strewn as it rims fine cliffs bordering Coire an Fhir-Leith on the left.

The well-won summit rewards with breathtaking views along the lengths of Loch Etive and Glen Etive, and the previously hidden south-east and south-west ridges lead the eye down to the remote country on the eastern shores of Loch Etive. The route onward takes the east ridge, the finest and most interesting of all, which is reached by following the rim of the summit plateau round to Ben Starav's lower eastern top and then keeping going. The ridge is a sharp arête of shattered rock that leads to the subsidiary top of Stob Coire Dheirg, and it calls for some easy and agreeable scrambling. Beyond the Stob, continue eastwards to descend steeply to the bealach below Glas Bheinn Mhor, then pick up a path on the left bank of the Allt nam Meirleach leading back to the Allt Mheuran and the outward route.

On the north ridge of Ben Starav.

23

	1	2	3	4	5
grade					
terrain					
navigation					
seriousness					

OS MAP: 50
GR: 271423
DISTANCE: 9½ miles (15km)
ASCENT: 970m (3,200ft)
TIME: 6½ hours

ASSESSMENT: a diverse circuit around of one of the great corries of the Central Highlands, whose rim varies from broad plateau to narrow rocky ridge.

SEASONAL NOTES: at its best under snow, when the eastern corrie is heavily corniced and at its most impressive, but Aonach Eagach will require care under such conditions. To avoid Aonach Eagach, bear south-eastwards down the western arm of the south-eastern corrie.

Stob Ghabhar is the finest mountain in the twisting Black Mount range that borders Rannoch Moor on the south-west, its pointed summit lying at the hub of a number of ridges that provide good walking above deep corries. The best route combines a round of the great eastern corrie (marked Coirein Lochain on the OS Landranger map) with a descent of the attractive south-eastern corrie (Coire na Muic).

Begin at Forest Lodge, 3½ miles (6km) from Bridge of Orchy on the A8005, and follow a Land Rover track westwards to old Clashgour schoolhouse, a corrugated metal building that is now Glasgow University Mountaineering Club's hut. Turn right here and follow an excellent stalkers' path up the left bank (right side) of the Allt Toaig into Coire Toaig. When the path peters out beside a series of waterfalls just short of the bealach between Stob Ghabhar and Stob a' Choire Odhair, continue up to the bealach for your first view of the eastern corrie, an immense bowl whose encircling cliffs rise 400m (1,300ft) to Stob Ghabhar's summit plateau.

Descend slightly to contour across the corrie's entrance to the far side. A short detour to the lochan at the heart of the corrie will reveal its true scale; in winter this is a truly spectacular spot. Gain the corrie's northern rim (Sron nan Giubhas) by veering right and climbing up steeply at the point of least resistance. The rim begins as a knobbly ridge but soon broadens out onto the extensive summit plateau, which curves round above the corrie to the summit. The summit cairn is perched close to the edge of the upper couloir, a classic ice route first climbed in 1897.

Heading from the summit, continue around the corrie to follow the southern rim out onto the most interesting section of the route – the narrow ridge of Aonach Eagach. While nowhere near as exciting as its Glen Coe namesake, this short, airy crest still calls for some simple scrambling in a fine situation. After the ridge broadens out, descend into the south-eastern corrie when convenient, and follow the burn down on steep grass beside a fine waterfall to regain the track along the Allt Toaig.

Note: for strong walkers who can arrange transport at both ends, the complete traverse of the Black Mount, from White Corries (GR 266524) in the north to Forest Lodge in the south, is a classic high-level expedition in either direction. The route follows the spine of the range across the summits of Meall a' Bhuiridh, Clach Leathad, Aonach Mor and Stob Ghabhar, without once dropping below 730m (2,400ft). A north-to-south traverse enables those who wish to gain height effortlessly to use the White Corries chairlift.

Stob Ghabhar from the Abhainn Shira.

	1	2	3	4	5
grade					
terrain					
navigation					
seriousness					

OS MAP: 41
GR: 081580
DISTANCE: 10 miles (16km)
ASCENT: 1,340m (4,400ft)
TIME: 7½ hours

ASSESSMENT: a scramble of great character followed by a classic horseshoe ridge walk.

SEASONAL NOTES: an exhilarating winter traverse for those competent on iced rock and narrow snow ridges. The steep descent into Gleann a' Chaolais may give problems under snow. The difficult north-east ridge of Sgorr Bhan can be avoided, if necessary, by an ascent of the easy north ridge.

The entrance to Loch Leven at the western end of Glen Coe is dominated by the craggy hump of Sgorr Dhonuill and its more graceful neighbour Sgorr Dhearg, which together with their outliers form a commanding horseshoe of peaks known collectively as Beinn a' Bheithir. The beithir was a destructive serpent, but the mountain today shows no trace of his deeds and provides an attractive traverse with fine coastal views.

The approach to the summits is hampered by gross afforestation in the northern corries, and the normal Munro bagger's route from Glennachulish requires precise route-finding if use of a machete is to be avoided. A much finer approach is that from Ballachulish village, which entails a short road walk at the end of the day but more than compensates for this by the beauty and interest of the ascent route.

Begin at Ballachulish village 1½ miles (2km) west of Glen Coe village on the A82. Take the street signposted 'Public Footpath to Glen Creran', which runs up the left bank (right side) of the River Laroch to a farmyard. From the road end an old track continues to Glen Creran past the foot of the north-east ridge of Sgorr Bhan, a magnificent ridge that has a real mountaineering ambience about it. Climb its crest, which narrows to a rocky arête and breaks out into several short steep pitches that call for easy but invigorating scrambling (mostly avoidable if necessary).

From Sgorr Bhan a ridge curves round to Sgorr Dhearg in a perfect arc that provides an

exquisite aerial passage; when corniced the symmetry of its unbroken line is breathtaking. Beyond Sgorr Dhearg a long easy-angled descent to a bealach is followed by a steeper climb up to Sgorr Dhonuill. Half-way up, a side ridge branches off to the rock tower of Sgorr a' Chaolais, which those with excess energy will find a sporting scramble well worthy of their attention. The final slopes of Sgorr Dhonuill provide further easy scrambling.

To complete the traverse of Beinn a' Bheithir, continue round the head of Gleann a' Chaolais. Between these two rises, which are given spot heights of 824 and 759 on the map, a grass gully enables a descent to the glen, where a path follows the left bank of the stream through the upper reaches of the forest to a forest road. Turn right along the road. Ignore a short left fork to a quarry then keep going straight on, ignoring tracks that join first from the right then twice from the left. The track eventually contours out of Gleann a' Chaolais and gives excellent views across Loch Leven as it descends to the roadside a short distance from Ballachulish village.

Perfect winter conditions on the ridge between Sgorr Bhan and Sgorr Dhearg.

	1	2	3	4	5
grade					
terrain					
navigation					
seriousness					

OS MAP: 41
GR: 171514
DISTANCE: 5½ miles (9km)
ASCENT: 1,050m (3,450ft)
TIME: 5½ hours

ASSESSMENT: a relentless ascent of The Wee Buachaille leads to an attractive ridge walk parallel to its neighbour The Big Buachaille (Buachaille Etive Mor) across the glen.

SEASONAL NOTES: providing the steep ascent causes no problems under snow, the remainder of the route develops into a good introduction to winter ridge walking. On the initial steep descent from the summit of Stob Dubh in the direction of Stob Coire Raineach, a beautiful cornice forms and may give problems.

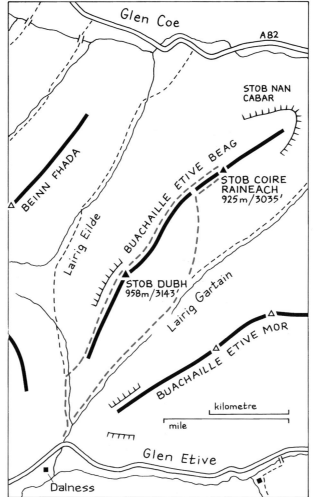

Between Bidean nam Bian and Buachaille Etive Mor in Glen Coe (Routes 8 and 9 in *50 Best Routes*), the less frequented Buachaille Etive Beag (The Wee Buachaille) rises in splendid isolation a full 470m (1,550ft) above its two deep, flanking passes – the Lairig Eilde and the Lairig Gartain. The mountain consists of two tops linked by a ridge that is pleasantly narrow without requiring any scrambling, and it would be more popular were it not for its more exalted neighbours. The north top (Stob Coire Raineach) is buttressed by a craggy spur (Stob nan Cabar) that deters access when viewed from the Glen Coe road, but the southern flanks of the mountain rise in one bold swoop from Glen Etive to the southern and higher top (Stob Dubh) and provide the key to the ascent.

Begin at the foot of the two passes near Dalness. The Lairig Eilde path goes up the left side of the river, which can be crossed at any of several points to gain the south-south-west ridge of the Buachaille. The best line keeps left at all path junctions, close by a fence that rises up the glen; at the end of the fence a side path curves round above an obvious tiered waterfall to reach the ridge.

The route to the summit needs no further description – it goes straight up, and your legs will soon be in no doubt that there is nothing wee about The Wee Buachaille. Fortunately it is worth the occasional halt for the magnificent view down Glen Etive to Loch Etive. Steep grass eventually gives way to an awkward

boulderfield through which a stony path zig-zags up to the level summit ridge of Stob Dubh, a delightful spot from which to view Stob Coire Raineach across a deep bealach. The interesting intervening ridge trends north-westwards, parallel to Buachaille Etive Mor's summit ridge across the Lairig Gartain. It is initially level for a few hundred metres, then it narrows and descends steeply to a twisting,

undulating section before another steep drop to the bealach. From here the craggy knob of Stob Coire Raineach, a new Munro in 1997, is easily reached, and you will certainly want to linger at the summit for the extensive panorama of Central Highland peaks strung out north of the Blackwater Reservoir. Those with energy to spare can improve the view along Glen Coe by walking out to Stob nan

Stob Dubh of Buachaille Etive Beag (left) and Stob na Broige of Buachaille Etive Mor (right).

Cabar located at the end of the ridge.

To descend, return to the bealach and go down easy grass slopes on the east to reach the Lairig Gartain path. This path leads up over the lairig and down past a series of waterfalls to your starting point.

	1	2	3	4	5
grade					
terrain					
navigation					
seriousness					

OS MAP: 41
GR: 143684
DISTANCE: 8 miles (13km)
ASCENT: 1,150m (3,750ft)
TIME: 6 hours

ASSESSMENT: a circuit of two contrasting mountains, combining an easy plateau stroll around the rim of a deep corrie on Mullach nan Coirean with the more awkward terrain and steeper ridges of Stob Ban – perhaps the shapeliest peak in the Mamores.

SEASONAL NOTES: under snow the route requires technical competence, especially the final section of the north-east ridge of Mullach nan Coirean and the descent of the east ridge of Stob Ban, whose junction with the south-west ridge may be corniced.

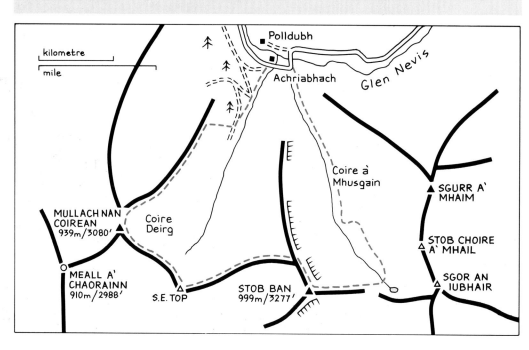

The narrow, twisting ridges of the Mamore range are characterised by excellent approach paths and some of the most enjoyable high-level ridge walking in the country. The range boasts a dozen or so tops and is large enough to yield a number of satisfying day walks. Routes 11 and 12 in *50 Best Routes* explore the central and eastern Mamores, but the two Munros of Mullach nan Coirean and Stob Ban at the western end of the range are of no less interest, and many consider Stob Ban to be the finest peak in the whole range.

The two neighbours could scarcely be more different. The Mullach has an undistinguished plateau summit but throws out some interesting ridges towards Glen Nevis, whereas Stob Ban is a contrasting and shapely cone that makes a picturesque backdrop to the view up Glen Nevis, its bold quartzite top often mistaken for a snowcap. The round of the two peaks makes a fine tramp best done from west to east in order to save the best until last.

Begin at Achriabhach Farm in Glen Nevis and take the excellent path, signposted 'Forest walk', that climbs along the perimeter of the forest and the banks of the Allt a' Choire Dheirg. The path crosses a forest road at a bend, rejoins it higher up and continues from 30m further along on the far side to a hillside seat. Climb the steep sparsely-wooded slopes above the seat to reach the Mullach's north-east ridge, then follow a path along the narrowing crest to the broad summit plateau. For those with energy to spare a short walk from here out to the south-west top of Meall a' Chaorainn gives a wonderful view over Loch Linnhe.

From the summit, follow the edge of the plateau around Coire Deirg to the south-east top, beyond which the plateau narrows to a ridge and a path scrambles over a rocky hump to the foot of Stob Ban's west ridge. The ascent of this ridge is straightforward at first but, after its junction with the north ridge, steep and awkward quartzite slopes have to be negotiated to gain the summit.

To complete the round, descend the east ridge of Stob Ban, which abuts sharply against the south-west ridge (easily missed in adverse weather). It leads down steeply at first before levelling off onto the bealach beneath Sgor an Iubhair. From the bealach, descend left into Coire a' Mhusgain and pick up a good stalkers' path that clings to the right bank of the gorge of the Allt Coire a' Mhusgain. The path provides a delightful descent beneath the crags of Stob Ban's east face and through an old stand of birch to reach the roadside near Achriabhach.

Stob Ban from the south-east Top of Mullach nan Coirean.

	1	2	3	4	5
grade					
terrain					
navigation					
seriousness					

OS MAP: 41
GR: 184778
DISTANCE: 11½ miles (18km)
ASCENT: 1,530m (5,000ft)
TIME: 8 hours

ASSESSMENT: a wild walk at 4,000ft (1,220m) amidst rock scenery of Alpine grandeur on the secret east side of the Big and Little Ridges.

SEASONAL NOTES: the ascent of the spur to Aonach Mor may be impracticable under snow, when the summits can be more easily gained by the Coire an t-Sneachda descent route. The summit slopes of Aonach Beag require care when iced. An Cul Choire and its environs are spectacular in winter and even more so in spring, when huge cornices rim the corrie.

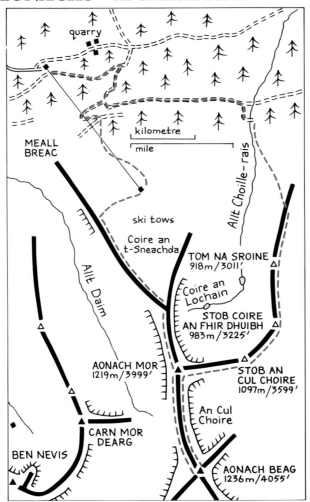

Between Ben Nevis and the Grey Corries (Routes 13 and 14 in *50 Best Routes*) lie the two fascinating high peaks of Aonach Mor and Aonach Beag. Aonach Beag (Little Ridge) is the sixth highest mountain in Britain and is in fact higher than Aonach Mor (Big Ridge), whose Gaelic name derives from its bulk rather than its height. They are wild and lonely mountains, especially so in the remote mountain fastness of their huge, magnificent eastern corries. The most interesting ascent route avoids the mechanised ski slopes in Coire an t-Sneachda on the north-west slopes of the Aonach Mor, and approaches the summits via an easterly ridge that sports three outlying Tops and gives wonderful views of the eastern corries.

The route begins at the skiers' car park at the end of the minor road, signposted Aonach Mor, that leaves the A82 north of Fort William. On the south side of the car park take the forest track that goes left beneath the gondola. At the first fork branch sharp right, at the next branch left and after a further 1½ miles (2km) branch right on a side track that climbs to a small dam on the Allt Choille-rais. Cross the dam and follow a developing path through birches on the right bank (left side) of the turbulent river to reach the forest fence, then climb relentless grass slopes to the summit of Tom na Sroine, the first Top.

Interest now increases as the well-defined ridge is followed over the second and third Tops, Stob Coire an Fhir Dhuibh and Stob an Cul Choire. Initially the Grey Corries and the

perfect bowl of Aonach Mor's Coire an Lochain command the attention, but increasingly glimpses of Aonach Beag's stupendous north-east corrie (An Cul Choire) spur you onwards. From the summit of Stob an Cul Choire this corrie is revealed in all its glory; the prominent rock ridge is the classic north-east ridge.

From Stob an Cul Choire, descend the fine rocky ridge that abuts against Aonach Mor and climb a steep spur to gain the summit plateau, bypassing a rock bluff on the right. From the flat mossy summit, gentle slopes lead down around the rim of An Cul Choire (great care in mist) to the steeper climb onto the dome of Aonach Beag. The views left into the corrie and right to Ben Nevis are spectacular.

Aonach Beag from across An Cul Choire.

To descend, return to Aonach Mor and cross the length of the summit plateau to the top of Coire an t-Sneachda. Descend the west rim to avoid the ski tows and follow the tourists' path across to the top gondola station, from where a path descends to the car park.

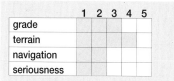

	1	2	3	4	5
grade					
terrain					
navigation					
seriousness					

OS MAP: 41
GR: 350782
DISTANCE: 10 miles (16km)
ASCENT: 1,040m (3,400ft)
TIME: 6½ hours

ASSESSMENT: a walk across the twin domes that tower over the Loch Treig trench, reached by an approach of unusual historical interest.

SEASONAL NOTES: in winter, steep snow may be encountered in several places. The ascent and descent of Stob Coire Easain especially should not be underestimated, especially as the summit slopes are often iced.

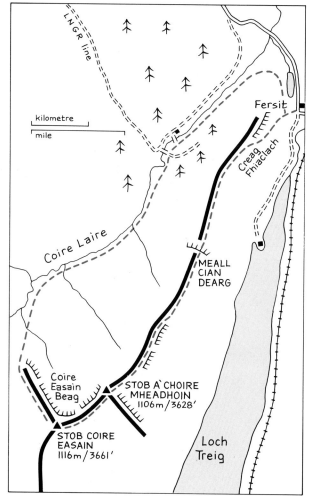

The twin Munros of Stob Coire Easain and Stob a' Choire Mheadhoin, known collectively as the Easains, stand in splendid isolation between Loch Treig to the east and the Lairig Leacach to the west. The Easain Mor (Big Waterfall) after which the higher Munro is named tumbles down the steep slopes above Loch Treigside. The ridge connecting the two peaks extends both north and south and provides a fine one-way walk from Corrour Station to Tulloch Station on the West Highland Railway; this can be made into a one-day trip by taking the morning train from Tulloch to Corrour. Even without using the train, the two peaks can be linked into a circuit of unusual interest from the north.

Begin at Fersit in Glen Spean, at the end of the minor road that leaves the A86 Loch Laggan road 5 miles (8km) east of Roybridge. Take the path on the right up to the line of the former Lochaber Narrow Gauge Railway (LNGR) and climb onto the ridge left of Creag Fhiaclach. Relatively level going leads to the foot of the craggy nose of Meall Cian Dearg, with Loch Treig stretching away to the left, and the West Highland Railway line incongruously hugging its shore. Pick a route straight up the nose to reach a level section of ridge whose unusually even turf gives wonderful walking. At the end of this section there is another rise to another level section before the final rise to Stob a' Choire Mheadhoin's stony summit.

The route onwards to Stob Coire Easain involves a steep, stony descent followed by a re-ascent of 150m (500ft) around the rim of Coire Easain Beag, whose slabby walls exhibit some impressive folding; the corrie rim is sometimes corniced well into early summer. From the summit of Stob Coire Easain, continue around the corrie rim on yet more steep, stony slopes that lead down into Coire Laire, where you will eventually come across a path on the right bank of the river. This path eventually meets the LNGR line, which takes you past some interesting old pipeline workings and along a delightfully easy track all the way back to Fersit.

The 19-mile (30km) LNGR was built in the 1920s to aid construction of a pipeline carrying water from Loch Treig to the aluminium works at Fort William. The Coire Lair intake, which captures the waters of the Allt Laire, was famous for its hairpin bend (GR 324774) and its still, which kept construction workers happy at their task. The line was gradually replaced by forest roads and eventually it was formally closed in 1971. There have been schemes to reopen the line for tourism, but so far nothing has been implemented.

The Easains from Lagganside.

	1	2	3	4	5
grade					
terrain					
navigation					
seriousness					

OS MAP: 42
GR: 547787
DISTANCE: 21 miles (34km)
ASCENT: 1,950m (6,400ft)
TIME: 14½ hours

Boathouse approach (each way):
5½ miles (9km), **out** 150m
(450ft) **back** 50m (150ft), 2 hrs
Ascent from Boathouse:
15 miles (25km), 1,750m
(5,750ft), 10½ hrs

ASSESSMENT: a long and
testing traverse of the narrow
ridges that radiate from one of

the most remote plateau
summits in the Highlands.

SEASONAL NOTES: in winter
narrow corniced ridges may be
encountered in several places,
and the Lancet Edge becomes
a serious proposition. Avoid the
summit plateau of Geal Charn
in foul winter weather.

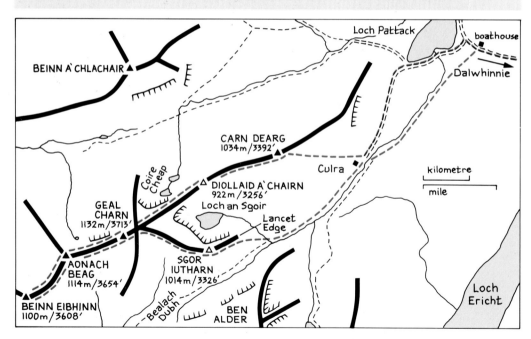

It is difficult to believe that any mountains in the Central Highlands could be as remote as 8 miles (13km) from the nearest public road as the eagle flies, yet such is the case with the high peaks of the Geal Charn group. Owing to the unenlightened access policy of recent estate owners and the closing of the Loch Ericht approach track to private transport, the shortest approach to the group is from Luiblea on Lagganside. The Loch Ericht approach, however, remains by far the best route and is described here in the hope that access improves. Until such times the route is a very long single-day route; many people cycle in, camp or stay at Culra bothy.

The approach is as for Ben Alder (Route 15 in *50 Best Routes*). From Dalwhinnie the track along Loch Ericht crosses the railway line south of the station; cars can be driven to a locked gate 1½ miles (2km) along. Branch right at Ben Alder Lodge to reach a shed (the Boathouse) near Loch Pattack. From here reach Culra bothy, either by taking the excellent stalkers' path across the moor and fording the Allt a' Chaoil-reidhe, or by taking the less pleasant Land Rover track that crosses the river (bridge nearby) on the south shore of Loch Pattack.

The mountains ahead are naturally divided into two groups by the deep gash of the Bealach Dubh; to the left is Ben Alder and to the right are the four Munros of the Geal Charn group. The summit of Geal Charn itself lies well back at the end of an extensive plateau; what immediately catches the eye is Sgor Iutharn and

its north-west ridge (the Lancet Edge), which drops to meet the path.

From Culra a path continues into the jaws of the Bealach Dubh. Leave it after crossing the burn coming down from Loch an Sgoir and climb the Lancet Edge direct. As height is gained, the ridge narrows to a rocky crest, which provides mild and pleasant scrambling in a fine situation above the moors of the approach route. Beyond the Lancet Edge lie Sgor Iutharn and the grassy plateau of Geal Charn. The summit cairn is at the north-west edge of the plateau and beyond it is a fine walk along a narrowing ridge, reminiscent of the Mamores, which undulates across Aonach Beag and curves round gracefully to the summit of Beinn Eibhinn.

To return, retrace your steps along the ridge

Approaching Culra, with Ben Alder (left) and Lancet Edge (right).

as far as Geal Charn then keep going north-eastwards down the sharp ridge (difficult to locate in mist) that separates Loch Coire Cheap from Loch an Sgoir. Continue over Diollaid a' Chairn to reach Carn Dearg then descend to Culra to rejoin the approach route.

	1	2	3	4	5
grade					
terrain					
navigation					
seriousness					

OS MAP: 34 or 42
GR: 483873
DISTANCE: 10 miles (16km)
ASCENT: 910m (3,000ft)
TIME: 6½ hours

ASSESSMENT: a walk amid impressive cliff and corrie scenery in the hidden recesses of a complex and majestic mountain.

SEASONAL NOTES: the mountain holds a lot of snow and Coire Ardair is a supreme winter climbing area, with its several posts providing testing ascents. The summit plateau and the environs of Coire Ardair demand great respect in winter and spring, and the section from the corrie to the Window is especially prone to avalanche.

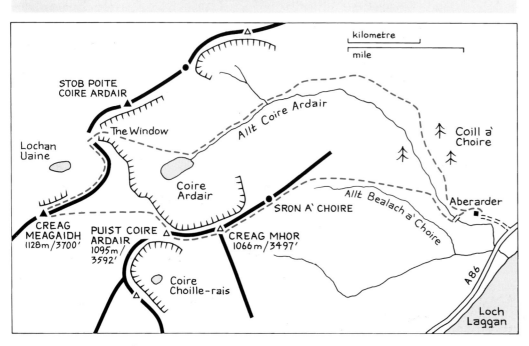

Seen from afar, Creag Meagaidh's seemingly tame topography does not prepare one for the scale and grandeur of the secluded corries that hide within its many recesses. Coire Ardair especially is one of the hidden gems of the Scottish Highlands. Its cliffs are 1½ miles (2km) long and up to 450m (1,500ft) high, and its towering buttresses are split by great gullies (called posts).

Yet, despite its splendour and its designation as a Site of Special Scientific Interest, Creag Meagaidh was saved from the ravages of commercial afforestation only by its purchase by the Nature Conservancy Council (now Scottish Natural Heritage) in 1985. The whole sorry affair was unfortunately only one example of the crying need for a land policy that will preserve the wild land of Scotland for the future. For the moment Creag Meagaidh is safe, however, and its delightful recesses await those who are prepared to expend a little energy.

Begin at the SNH car park at Aberarder Farm on the A86 Loch Laggan road. Follow the track to the farm and the continuing path up the right-hand side of the gracefully curving glen, passing through the fine birch woods of Coill a' Choire. The great cliffs of Coire Ardair soon come into view and loom ever more impressively as the path approaches the lochan-filled hollow at its heart.

The route to the summit plateau traverses right beneath the cliffs to the curious nick in the skyline known as the Window. At the Window turn left to climb onto the extensive summit plateau. A large cairn is reached, and the true summit lies a short distance beyond, near the edge of cliffs above Lochan Uaine.

A return via the southern of Coire Ardair's two protecting arms provides a high-level ridge walk that reveals yet more aspects of the cliffs and the mountain. Head back across the plateau to the corrie rim (great care required in mist) and continue round the cliff edge, with spectacular views of the lochan far below. A well-defined ridge leads over Puist Coire Ardair to the fine viewpoint of Creag Mhor, from where it is worth descending southwards for a short distance to view the perfect bowl of Coire Choille-rais (Moy Corrie on OS map) with its own cliff-girt lochan, the perfect partner to Coire Ardair.

To reach Aberarder, descend over Sron a' Choire into the shallow corrie drained by the Allt Bealach a' Choire, keeping left of the burn and making for a path beside the remains of an old fence that runs diagonally across the moor to the Allt Coire Ardair. From here a path leads down beside the river to a bridge and so to Aberarder.

In the claustrophobic confines of Coire Ardair beneath the Window.

	1	2	3	4	5
grade					
terrain					
navigation					
seriousness					

OS MAP: 40/49
GR: 929597
DISTANCE: 7½ miles (12km)
ASCENT: 1,310m (4,300ft)
TIME: 7½ hours

ASSESSMENT: a corrie skyline circuit that explores the many aspects of an impressive and unjustly ignored rock peak.

SEASONAL NOTES: in winter, steep snow slopes on either side of the Bealach Feith an Amean are not for the inexperienced, and it may be best to ascend via

the descent route. Routefinding on the descent from the summit to the south-east summit is difficult and demands extreme caution in adverse weather.

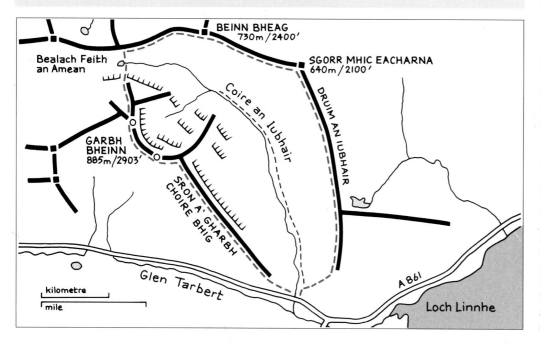

The mountainous district of Ardgour is cut off from the popular playgrounds of Glen Coe and Glen Nevis by the long sea inlet of Loch Linnhe. The Corran ferry crosses the loch but, as there are no Munros to be climbed, the area remains relatively quiet. Its long, lonely glens and rugged mountains are well worth exploring, however, and none more so than Garbh Bheinn, the great rock peak that is prominent in the view across Loch Linnhe. The rock buttresses of Garbh Bheinn's north-east face dominate the upper reaches of Coire an Iubhair and make the round of the corrie sky-line the best route in Ardgour, with plenty of opportunities for scrambling amidst the impressive rock scenery.

Begin at the car park on the east side of the bridge over the Abhain Coire an Iubhair, in Glen Tarbert, on the A861. Climb steep, tussocky grass slopes to gain Druim an Iubhair, the broad and complex ridge, dotted with lochans, that swings gradually left around the corrie to the summit of Sgor Mhic Eacharna. Across the corrie, the north-east face of Garbh Bheinn becomes ever more impressive. Dropping 300m (1,000ft) directly from the summit to the corrie floor is the Great Ridge, first climbed in 1897. To its immediate north is the Great Gully, at one time a notorious 'last great problem', not climbed until 1946. Further right is the four-tiered north-east buttress, whose third tier contains the Leac Mhor, a huge slab, said to be the biggest in Scotland, measuring approximately 150m (500ft) by 90m (300ft).

Beyond Sgor Mhic Eacharna the terrain becomes increasingly rocky. A steep descent and re-ascent is required to gain Beinn Bheag, and then the ridge narrows attractively above wild glens to both north and south. Continue along the ridge until it swings right at a rocky knoll and from here descend steep grass rakes among outcrops to the Bealach Feith an Amean, at the head of Coire an Iubhair. Garbh Bheinn rises directly above. From the lochan in the jaws of the bealach, go straight up a steep grass gully, which cuts through the cliffs to reach the rim of the fine north-west corrie, whose slabby walls have an almost Cuillin grandeur. Clamber up the left-hand skyline, with ample opportunity for scrambling on the excellent gneiss, to reach the summit.

Descend around the cliff edge, which curves

Garbh Bheinn from across Loch Linnhe.

left to the south-east top; there are traces of a path but take care in mist not to cut left too soon. Continue south-eastwards down the long rocky ridge of Sron a' Gharbh Choire Bhig, which offers stunning views over island-studded Loch Linnhe, to complete the circuit of Coire an Iubhair.

	1	2	3	4	5
grade					
terrain					
navigation					
seriousness					

OS MAP: 40
GR: 765816
DISTANCE: 11½ miles (18km)
ASCENT: 1,640m (5,400ft)
TIME: 9 hours

ASSESSMENT: a long and lonely ridge walk across craggy terrain with magnificent West Coast views that will be long remembered.

SEASONAL NOTES: a fine winter tramp, of testing length if the complete route is attempted. Steep snow slopes may be encountered as the ridge progresses, but the early tops should give few problems.

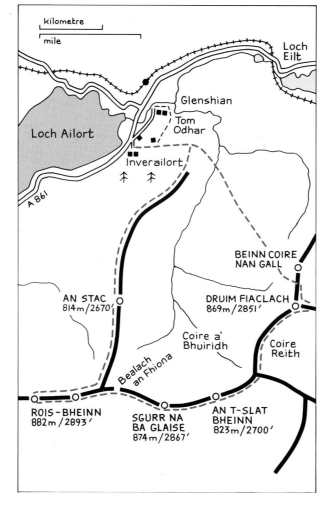

The district of Moidart, which stretches from Loch Shiel to the Sound of Arisaig, is surrounded by green loch-filled glens and rendered easily accessible by the West Highland Railway and the 'Road to the Isles' from Fort William to Mallaig. Yet the interior is wild and remote, and the traverse of Rois-Bheinn and its satellites, though never reaching Munro height, is one of the finest ridge walks in the Western Highlands. Large amounts of bare rock enliven the traverse of the ridge, which is winding, undulating, complex and constantly interesting.

Begin at the start of the minor road, signposted Glenshian, 700 metres south of the junction of the A830 and A861 at Lochailort (take care not to cause an obstruction or disturbance). The road forks immediately. Walk up the right branch and go left on a track in front of Inverailort cottages and across fields. When the track turns left at an old building, take the path that goes straight on up the defile right of Tom Odhar onto the open moor. When the path ends, cross the Allt a' Bhuiridh and make a fairly steep rising traverse across the tussocky slopes of Beinn Coire nan Gall to the lochan at the bealach below Druim Fiaclach. Steep grass slopes then lead up among outcrops to this first top on the main ridge.

The route to Rois-Bheinn goes south-west, but first wander out to the end of the east ridge, which gives Druim Fiaclach (Toothed Ridge) its name, where sharp folds of rock thrust out of the ground like sharks' fins and make pleasant scrambling. From the summit, follow the south-west ridge as it snakes around the rim of the craggy headwall of Coire Reith and turns south to descend steeply to a bealach; a path meanders among the outcrops. Beyond the bealach the ridge twists westwards once more, over rocky terrain dotted with lochans (confusing in mist), to reach the grassy top of An t-Slat-bheinn. Outcrops now give way to boulders as the ridge leads over Sgurr na Ba Glaise and down to the Bealach an Fhiona for the final climb up to Rois-Bheinn.

Rois-Bheinn's east and higher top is reached first, but the short stroll out to the west top is a must for the magnificent view of the western seascape, across the Sound of Arisaig to the Inner Hebrides (of which you have been afforded only tantalising glimpses during the course of the traverse). To descend, return to the Bealach an Fhiona and go down northwards to a lower bealach below the rocky hump of An Stac. To complete the round of Coire a' Bhuiridh and prolong the westward view, traverse An Stac to regain the path beside Tom Odhar back to your starting point.

Druim Fiaclach from the Prince's Cairn on the Mallaig road.

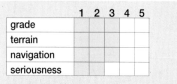

Route 18: STREAP • THE WESTERN HIGHLANDS

	1	2	3	4	5
grade					
terrain					
navigation					
seriousness					

OS MAP: 40
GR: 931799
DISTANCE: 10 miles (16km)
ASCENT: 1,070m (3,500ft)
TIME: 6½ hours

ASSESSMENT: an ascent of a very attractive peak, and a good introduction, involving some very mild scrambling, to the pleasures of narrow ridges.

SEASONAL NOTES: in winter, steep snow may be encountered on the ascent to the Bealach Coire nan Cearc. Snow also transforms the summit ridges of Streap into graceful snow arêtes, which look beautiful, but which should be left well alone by the inexperienced.

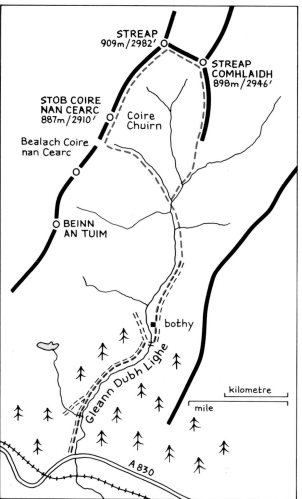

The Locheil District west of Fort William contains a number of fine hill walks on mountains that hide their considerable attractions far from prying eyes at the end of long, forested glens. The best circuit in the area is the Corryhully Horseshoe, described in Route 16 in *50 Best Routes*, but the best-looking mountain is the wonderfully named Streap (Climbing), whose narrow south-west ridge is perhaps the finest feature in the area.

Streap is separated from the Corryhully Horseshoe to the west by a deep bealach, while to the east is an even deeper bealach. This isolation makes the mountain the high point of a long, steep-sided north-south ridge that contains a whole series of distinct tops, five of which are over 800m (2,600ft) high. The circular route described here takes in the highest section of this ridge, which crosses Streap's pointed summit.

Begin at the bridge over the Dubh Lighe on the A830, 2 miles (3km) east of Glenfinnan, and take the forest road up the right bank (left side) of the river beside some attractive pools and cascades. The track runs up the glen for 2½ miles (4km). Keep right at a fork after 15 minutes, and at a junction immediately after the first sighting of Gleann Dubh Lighe bothy, branch right on a side track that crosses the river (bridge) and continues until ½ mile (1km) beyond the bothy. From the end of the track, the old path that it has replaced continues up the glen to a ruined shieling in Coire Chuirn. This is a fine spot, with the rocky peaks of

Streap and its satellites towering all around. From here, climb directly to the Bealach Coire nan Cearc, keeping close to one of the burns that descend from it to avoid slabs.

At the bealach, the ridge proper begins with an ascent among outcrops to the summit of Stob Coire nan Cearc. From here the final section of Streap's south-west ridge looks exceedingly sharp, and the pleasant stroll to its foot gains from anticipation. On closer inspection, however, the ascent turns out to be easier than it looks, having some fine situations but requiring only elementary handwork.

From the summit a short steep descent south-eastwards leads to another narrow section, bypassed by a path on the left, although again of no difficulty. The descent continues interestingly to a dip before a steep re-ascent gains the grassy dome of Streap Comhlaidh. The ridge between Streap and Streap Comhlaidh encloses the steep headwall of Coire Chuirn, whose unstable rock and fallen debris are evidence of an enormous landslip here. Regain the ruined shieling and approach path in Coire Chuirn by descending the steep south ridge of Streap Comhlaidh.

Streap from Stob Coire nan Cearc.

	1	2	3	4	5
grade					
terrain					
navigation					
seriousness					

OS MAP: 33
GR: 029030
DISTANCE: 7 miles (11km)
ASCENT: 1,130m (3,700ft)
TIME: 5½ hours

ASSESSMENT: a pleasant walk along a broad ridge around the rim of a series of grand and rugged corries, reached by perhaps the best mountain path in the Western Highlands.

SEASONAL NOTES: in winter, when the zigzagging paths are obliterated by snow, steep snow is likely to be encountered on the summit slopes of Gleouraich and the crossing of the Fiar Bealach. Cornices on the several corrie rims vie to win The Most Beautiful Cornice competition.

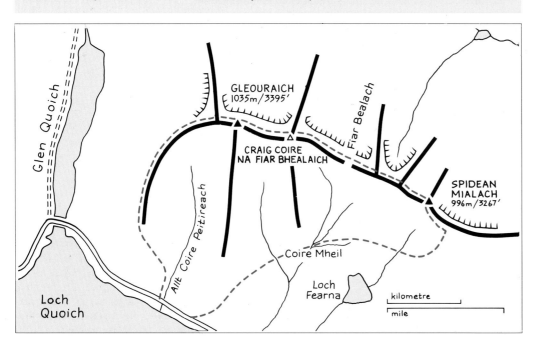

The great scalloped mountains of Gleouraich and Spidean Mialach, whose hidden north sides have been gouged out into a series of great corries, rise directly from the roadside on the north shore of Loch Quoich. Their lochside slopes are uniformly grassy, but an ascent from this side uses perhaps the finest stalkers' path in the country to give access to a fine 2 mile (3km) long ridge walk that links the two summits via the very rim of the northern corries.

Begin just west of the Allt Coire Peitireach, 1 mile (1½ km) east of Quoich Bridge. A roadside cairn marks the start of the stalkers' path, built to serve Glenquoich Lodge before it was inundated beneath the waters of the enlarged loch; the overgrown rhododendrons here are all that remain of the former lodge gardens. The excellent path climbs away from the Allt Coire Peitireach to make a series of rising zigzags onto the south-west ridge of Gleouraich, with wonderful views opening up over Loch Quoich. Higher up, the path contours left around a hump in the ridge, above airy drops into Glen Quoich, and ends at the foot of the steep summit slopes of Gleouraich. A boot-worn path continues up among grass and boulders to join the north ridge at the edge of the first of the northern corries, and the summit is not far beyond.

The route onwards to Spidean Mialach continues in a series of sweeping arcs around the northern corrie rims, the result of spur ridges that jut northwards between the corries.

The first arc crosses stony ground to the subsidiary top of Craig Coire na Fiar Bhealaich, and then steeper ground, negotiated by another excellent zigzagging path, leads down to the Fiar Bealach between the two Munros. Three more arcs lead up to the summit of Spidean Mialach. The first is steep; either keep to the stony crest for the view or climb easier grass slopes to the right. After this the gradient eases to the summit. The three spurs that jut northwards to end each arc are narrow, rocky and interesting. The second especially is extremely narrow and drops into remote Glen Loyne in a series of steps on which scramblers will find good sport.

The direct, steep, stony descent from Spidean Mialach into Coire Mheil can be outflanked by descending easy grass slopes from

The summit of Spidean Mialach.

the next dip in the ridge and contouring back to the small saddle above Loch Fearna. Follow the stream that descends from the saddle to the Allt a' Mheil and cross to pick up another stalkers' path that, although boggy in places, descends pleasantly to the roadside only a few minutes walk from your starting point.

	1	2	3	4	5
grade					
terrain					
navigation					
seriousness					

OS MAP: 33
GR: 044114
DISTANCE: 6 miles (10km)
ASCENT: 900m (2,950ft)
TIME: 5½ hours

ASSESSMENT: a round of the 'trembling' ridges on the south side of Glen Shiel – one of the most sporting, yet one of the most ignored rounds in the glen.

SEASONAL NOTES: under snow, the steepness of the ascent of the north end of Aonach air Chrith should not be underestimated, and narrow snow arêtes and iced rocks may greatly increase the difficulty of the traverse of A' Chioch and Druim a' Ciche. The descent towards Maol Chinn-dearg may also require extra care.

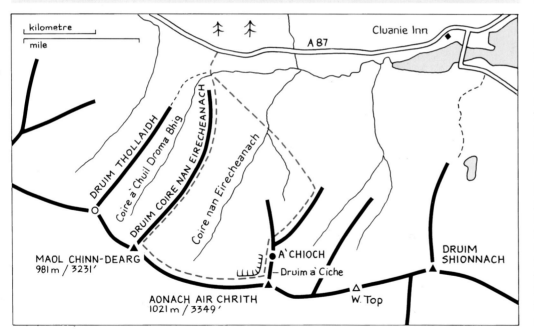

The South Glen Shiel Ridge links no less than seven Munros and provides a magnificent ridge walk for those fit enough to tackle it, but the most interesting ridge on the south side of the glen is ironically a side ridge, Druim a' Ciche (Ridge of the Breast), which branches off the main ridge and is unjustly ignored. This ridge connects the summit of Aonach air Chrith (Trembling Ridge) with its north top (A' Chioch, The Breast) and, when combined with the most narrow section of the main ridge to Maol Chinn-dearg, gives one of the best rounds in Glen Shiel.

Begin 2 miles (3km) west of Cluanie Inn on the A87, just beyond a right-hand bend where a road sign warns of rockfall danger (lay-by just beyond). From beside the sign a stalkers' path descends to boggy flats at the foot of Coire a' Chuil Droma Bhig and then goes left across a stream to climb Druim Coire nan Eirecheanach. This path will be the route of descent, but for the moment leave it at the first zigzag and continue left across the moor around the foot of Druim Coire nan Eirecheanach.

Cross the stream that drains the next corrie (Coire nan Eirecheanach) and climb direct the grassy hump that marks the end of Aonach air Chrith's north-east ridge, avoiding crags higher up. It is a steep, relentless climb – with not even a cairn at the top to salute your progress – but the promise of the rocky skyline ahead will lure you ever upwards. Once over the hump, steep, boulder-strewn slopes lead up to A' Chioch and the first easy scramble of the day across its sharp summit crest. A short dip follows and then two rock bluffs stand astride the connecting ridge (Druim a' Ciche) to the main summit. They look daunting but both go direct, involving slightly exposed but straightforward and enjoyable scrambling, although all the fun can be bypassed on the right if necessary. You finish on a high rock platform just before Aonach air Chrith's grassy summit dome. The summit is the third Munro on the South Glen Shiel Ridge, and you now follow a path along the ridge, around the rim of Coire nan Eirecheanach, to the fourth Munro, Maol Chinn-dearg.

The initial descent around the cliff edge calls for some elementary handwork but, beyond a saddle, the path becomes a staircase in the grass and provides a very pleasant walk. To complete the round of the corrie, descend Druim Coire nan Eirecheanach, which is Maol Chinn-dearg's well-defined and pleasantly grassy north-east ridge. Further down, the well-engineered stalker's path that you left at its beginning provides a painless descent back to the roadside.

On the ridge between Aonach air Chrith and Maol Chinn-dearg.

	1	2	3	4	5
grade					
terrain					
navigation					
seriousness					

OS MAP: 33
GR: 090121
DISTANCE: 8 miles (13km)
ASCENT: 1,000m (3,300ft)
TIME: 6½ hours

ASSESSMENT: a good ridge walk on a retiring but attractive mountain, firstly on an unusual narrow grass ridge and then on an even narrower rock ridge. Very steep grass slopes make the route best avoided when wet.

SEASONAL NOTES: the south ridge of Ciste Dhubh becomes corniced and spectacular in winter, requiring technical competence. Am Bathach may also provide some sport, depending on the condition of the snow on the steep ascent and the narrowness of the snow ridge above.

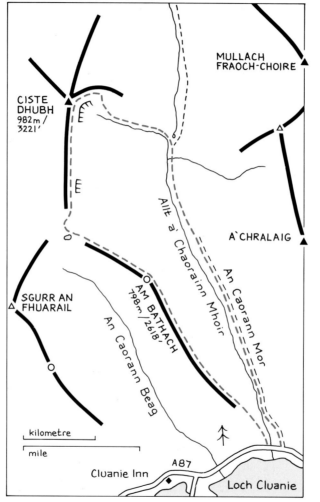

Of the many fine mountains enclosing Glen Shiel, Ciste Dhubh is the most retiring. It lies to the north of the glen half hidden behind the grassy lump of Am Bathach, yet anyone who catches a glimpse of its soaring summit will be drawn to it. And who could resist the lure of its sinister name (meaning Black Chest or Black Coffin)?

The shortest approach climbs the defile of An Caorann Beag to the Bealach a' Choinich at the foot of the south ridge, but it is more interesting to go over the grassy lump of Am Bathach on the right of the defile for views of the mountain, and for Am Bathach's unique summit – a narrow grass ridge that seems totally out of place among the rocky Glen Shiel mountains.

Begin 50 metres west of the bridge over the Allt a' Chaorainn Mhoir, 1 mile (1½km) east of Cluanie Inn on the A87. A path begins at a gate in a fence and climbs straight up the steep grass slopes ahead to Am Bathach's tapering summit ridge; the summit is the second of two tops.

Grass slopes continue down to the boggy Bealach a' Choinich, a confusing place in mist owing to hummocky terrain and the bealach's position at the head of not two, but three glens. From the bealach a very steep grass slope climbs to the south ridge of Ciste Dhubh. Seek out the path on the far left, beside a prominent rock outcrop, to find the easiest angle. The ridge rises and narrows to a knob of rock, well seen from Am Bathach, that marks the start of the eastern cliffs and the most entertaining part of the route. The cliff edge is quite narrow for a while, though without difficulty; a path goes along the crest and another path, for vertigo sufferers, traverses lower down. The two paths meet beyond the narrow section. Further along, the ridge narrows again along the clifftop as it crosses a shallow dip and rises more steeply to the summit of Ciste Dhubh; again the path is well established and without difficulty.

From the summit perch, easier grass slopes lead onward around the cliff edge, and then an awkward steepening, dangerous when wet, takes you down to the east ridge. On reaching a shallow dip beyond the summit crags, cut back right into the upper eastern corrie to avoid further steep slopes lower down. Follow the stream down to the Allt a' Chaorainn Mhoir and pick up a path on the left bank that becomes a rough track down the defile of An Caorann Mor, reaching the roadside 200 metres from your starting point.

Ciste Dhubh and Am Bathach from across Glen Shiel.

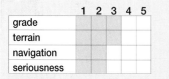

	1	2	3	4	5
grade					
terrain					
navigation					
seriousness					

OS MAP: 33
GR: 092121
DISTANCE: 8 miles (13km)
ASCENT: 1,110m (3,650ft)
TIME: 6 hours

ASSESSMENT: a ridge walk across two contrasting mountains, one massive and one airy, which includes the negotiation of the most pinnacled ridge in the Glen Shiel hills. **NB** the route is graded 3, but a direct traverse of the pinnacles is Grade 5.

SEASONAL NOTES: a major winter mountaineering expedition; along the narrow ridge rising to Mullach Fraoch-choire there sometimes forms a fragile cornice that is one of the most beautiful in the Highlands.

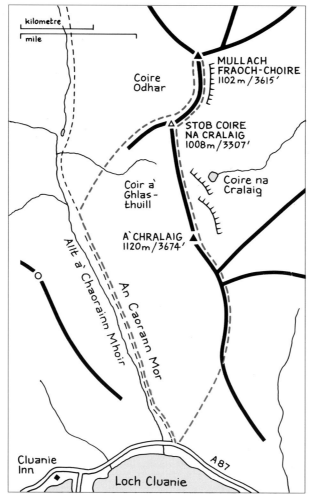

The unsung peak of Mullach Fraoch-choire is well hidden from the Glen Shiel roadside by its bulky neighbour A' Chralaig, yet its tapering, pinnacled summit ridge deserves to be better known. The traverse of the two mountains gives a sporting route of many contrasts.

Begin where Route 21 ends, at the foot of An Caorann Mor, near the west end of Loch Cluanie on the A87. Climb beside a stream directly up the steep grassy hillside to reach the skyline on the broad south ridge of A' Chralaig. Turn left to follow the increasingly stony ridge across a welcome level section and up to a shoulder, from where a steep side ridge drops away to the right. The main ridge bears left and passes another ridge on the right before rising to the massive summit cairn.

Things now become much more interesting as the ridge snakes its way northwards to the small pointed top of Stob Coire na Cralaig. It is initially straight, then it bears left at a rocky corner that requires a spot of handwork, and then it goes right and left again to descend to a bealach and rise to the summit of the Stob.

Another abrupt swing to the right now marks a turning point in the route's character as the ridge leads on to Mullach Fraoch-choire, whose sharp crest (seen ahead) starts to dominate all thoughts. The ridge narrows considerably, with a path along its crest, as it descends to a bealach and rises to a rocky point, and then it makes a final swing back to the left and breaks out into several pinnacles. The traverse of the pinnacles is a Grade 5 scramble, made to seem even

harder by the considerable exposure, and even the bypass path (which weaves among the pinnacles and gives this route its Grade 3 rating) is quite exposed, involves some handwork and requires care when muddy. Beyond the pinnacles a final straightforward rise leads to the summit of the Mullach, a fine pyramid point at the apex of three narrow ridges.

To return to your starting point without reversing the whole route, it is necessary to descend the steep western slopes of the mountain into An Caorann Mor. The easiest way off is to continue along the north-east ridge until you can descend easily on the left; a shorter route returns across the pinnacled ridge and descends steep stony slopes into Coire Odhar

Mullach Fraoch-choire from A' Chralaig.

from the bealach before Stob Coire na Cralaig. The most pleasant way down, however, is to climb back to the summit of the Stob and descend its south-west spur, contouring around the hillside lower down to pick up the track through An Caorann Mor.

	1	2	3	4	5
grade					
terrain					
navigation					
seriousness					

OS MAP: 25 or 33
GR: 981223
DISTANCE: 17 miles (27km)
ASCENT: 1,690m (5,550ft)
TIME: 10½ hours

ASSESSMENT: a good path leads through a rocky defile into remote country, where an isolated mountain of great character awaits the intrepid hillwalker.

SEASONAL NOTES: in winter the length of the approach walk and the steepness of the east ridge should not be underestimated. A beautiful but dangerous cornice forms between the summit and the west top. The steep grass slopes descending into Gleann Gniomhaidh can be unexpectedly awkward when wet or under snow.

North of the Glen Shiel hills, and separated from them by long and beautiful Glen Affric, is a country of wide horizons, where the mountains have a grandeur born of magnificent approaches and long high ridges rising above remote glens. Most of the hills are best approached via Glen Affric from the east, but the remote outlier of Sgurr nan Ceathreamhnan is best reached from the west. Like nearby Beinn Fhada, Sgurr nan Ceathreamhnan radiates a number of long ridges that support a cluster of subsidiary tops, but it is a more graceful mountain than its neighbour, with a narrow tent-shaped summit ridge that provides a fine ridge walk.

Of the many possible approach routes the best is that from Glen Elchaig via the mountain's long, narrow northern ridges, but this is currently impracticable owing to the unenlightened access policy of Glen Elchaig estate (locked gate on access road). Of the remaining approaches, that from Strath Croe at the head of Loch Duich is much the most interesting.

Begin at the Forestry Commission car park at Dorusduain (as for Beinn Fhada – Route 24 in *50 Best Routes*). Keep right on a Land Rover track, go through the gate to Dorusduain House and branch right just beyond on a path that crosses the Abhainn Chonaig (bridge) to join the path up Gleann Choinneachain. The path climbs into the wild rocky jaws of the Bealach an Sgairne, between the steep hillsides of A' Ghlas-bheinn and Beinn Fhada, and then

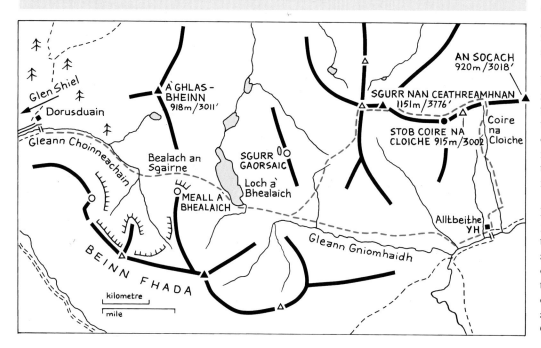

descends to the remote mountain sanctuary of Loch a' Bhealaich, as lonely and desolate a spot as you could wish to find. From here it continues down Gleann Gniomhaidh to the oasis in the wilderness that is Alltbeithe youth hostel (open in summer only). Vehicular access for stalking has reduced the latter stages of the path to mud in some places.

From Alltbeithe, a stalkers' path heads northwards up Coire na Cloiche to the bealach between Sgurr nan Ceathreamhnan and An Socach; this latter Munro (not named on OS map) can be easily bagged if desired. Turning westwards, the ridge climbs over Stob Coire na Cloiche and narrows over a couple of levellings to reach abruptly the cairn that crowns the east top and summit of Sgurr nan Ceathreamhnan. Beyond lies the narrow summit ridge that leads to the lower west top; although quite exposed in places and requiring some handwork on the crest, it is without difficulty and ends all too soon.

From the west top, follow the fence that descends the south ridge and bears right to the saddle below Sgurr Gaorsaic. From here, go down steep grass slopes on the south side of Sgurr Gaorsaic and contour right to rejoin the path along Gleann Gniomhaidh for the long walk back to Dorusduain.

The east ridge of Sgurr nan Ceathreamhnan.

	1	2	3	4	5
grade					
terrain					
navigation					
seriousness					

OS MAP: 25
GR: 040493
DISTANCE: 14 miles (23km)
ASCENT: 1,300m (4,250ft)
TIME: 8½ hours

ASSESSMENT: a typically wild and alluring West Highland ridge walk, on rough, narrow ridges in remote surroundings.

SEASONAL NOTES: in winter the steep mountainsides and ridges that guard the summits are no place for the inexperienced. Sgurr

Choinnich's summit ridge especially becomes heavily corniced in winter, and both this and the connection to Sgurr a' Chaorachain require care.

The head of Loch Monar is today a remote and lonely place, and climbing in the amphitheatre of mountains that enclose it has a wilderness feel to it, yet a thriving community once lived here. Most of the local inhabitants were evicted by the Highland Clearances of the 19th century, with the last nail in the coffin being provided by the raising of the water level when Loch Monar was dammed for hydro-electric power in 1960. Around the head of the loch are clustered four Munros and their satellites, which divide neatly into two groups to provide two exhilarating West Highland hill walks.

As the old track along the western reaches of Loch Monar now lies under water, the best approach to the hills is from Craig, 2½ miles (4km) east of Achnashellach on the A890, where a forest road crosses the railway line and the River Carron. Once over the river, keep left at the first fork and, higher up, keep left at another to emerge from the forest into a broad open glen where the Allt a' Chonais meanders beneath the broken west face of Sgurr nan Ceannaichean – a perfect hidden valley.

At the end of the plain the track veers left round a knoll towards Glenuaig Lodge; at this point fork right on a stalkers' path that crosses the river and meanders up to the Bealach Bhearnais at the foot of Sgurr Choinnich's west ridge. The route to the peaks on the south side of Loch Monar branches off here and is described later (see Route 25), while the north Loch Monar peaks are described here, beginning with the ascent of Sgurr Choinnich.

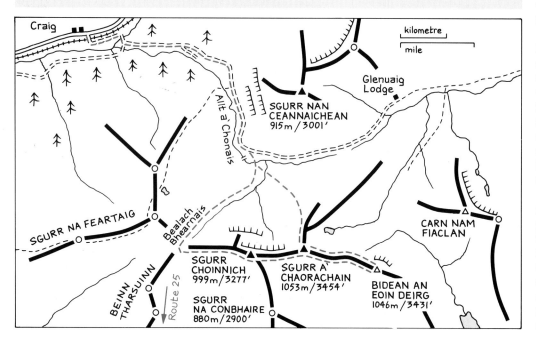

Sgurr Choinnich's west ridge is steep and broken by rock outcrops, which provide scrambling opportunities if taken direct. The final 200 metres follows the rim of the fine northern corrie to the castellated summit. From here a worthwhile detour can be made along the gentle south ridge to Sgurr na Conbhaire, a rarely visited peak that gives an eagle's view of Loch Monar. The dip between Sgurr Choinnich and Sgurr na Conbhaire is known as the Bowman's Pass (after the bowmen who hunted deer in these parts in the time of James VI of Scotland).

From Sgurr Choinnich a steep descent and re-ascent along a rough narrow ridge leads to Sgurr a' Chaorachain, beyond which a broad,

Sgurr a' Chaorachain from Sgurr Choinnich.

stony highway continues to Bidein an Eoin Deirg, the last top of the day perched high above Srath Mhuilich. The best way back is to return to Sgurr a' Chaorachain and descend its grassy north ridge, avoiding some outcrops, to reach the track back along the Allt a' Chonais.

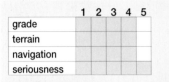

Route 25: BIDEIN A'CHOIRE SHEASGAICH AND LURG MHOR • WESTERN HIGHLANDS

	1	2	3	4	5
grade					
terrain					
navigation					
seriousness					

OS MAP: 25
GR: 040493
DISTANCE: 18½ miles (30km)
ASCENT: 1,900m (6,200ft)
TIME: 11½ hours

ASSESSMENT: a magnificent expedition with a real mountaineering flavour on two rugged and complex West Highland mountains; remote, long and exciting.

SEASONAL NOTES: a lengthy winter route whose many steep, narrow and rocky sections require technical competence on snow and iced rock. The major difficulties occur on the tiered north ridge of Bidein a' Choire Sheasgaich and the ridge between Lurg Mhor and Meall Mor.

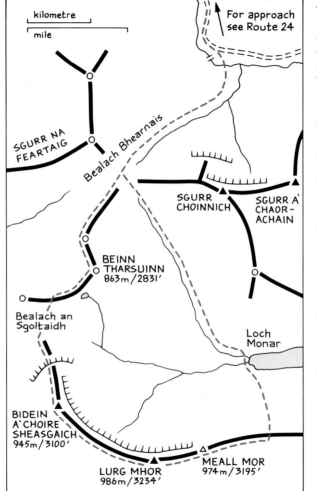

The traverse of Bidein a' Choire Sheasgaich and Lurg Mhor, the two peaks forming the southern arm of the amphitheatre of peaks that enclose the head of Loch Monar, is one of the finest expeditions in the Western Highlands. They are remote and contrasting mountains, Bidein, a crag-girt pointed cone, and Lurg Mhor, a long, relatively flat ridge, whose traverse turns out to be unexpectedly exciting.

The best approach to the mountains is from Craig via the Bealach Bhearnais (see Route 24). From the bealach, the route to Bidein is barred by Beinn Tharsuinn, a grassy lump of a hill that lies across the head of Loch Monar and whose Gaelic name (meaning Transverse Mountain) is doubly apt as it lies on the watershed between the east and west coasts of Scotland. There are no easy ways round Beinn Tharsuinn, and so it is necessary to climb over it in order to reach the narrow defile of the Bealach an Sgoltaidh at the foot of Bidein's rocky north ridge. The ascent from here involves some interesting route-finding problems as a route must be threaded through the tiers of cliffs that rise overhead. It is best to keep to the left, following the line of a prominent stone dyke built to channel deer into the bealach for the hunt. The first tier is broken and easy; the next goes by a gully on the left that veers to the right, reaching easier ground at the first of two sparkling lochans. From here a graceful tapering ridge leads to the summit.

Turning south-eastwards, easy ground descends around the rim of the craggy corrie that separates Bidein from Lurg Mhor. A re-ascent of 250m (800ft) is required to gain the summit of Lurg Mhor, and here the fun begins again. Lurg Mhor is connected to Meall Mor ½ mile (1km) away to the east by a narrow rocky ridge, which at one point has a short hiatus that involves an awkward move. There is no real difficulty, however, and this exhilarating scramble high above Loch Monar ends all too soon.

To avoid returning over Bidein a' Choire Sheasgaich and Beinn Tharsuinn continue down the gentle east ridge of Meall Mor for about 1 mile (1½km), until it is possible to make a steep descent to the head of Loch Monar. Once into the glen, pick up a good stalkers' path that climbs the left bank (right side) of the Allt Bealach Crudhain to the Bealach Bhearnais. Half-way up, the path suddenly ends, but the going remains good for the last weary climb to the bealach, where the stalkers' path leading back down to the Allt a' Chonais is rejoined.

Bidein a' Choire Sheasgaich from Beinn Tharsuinn.

Route 26: MAOILE LUNNDAIDH • THE WESTERN HIGHLANDS

	1	2	3	4	5
grade					
terrain					
navigation					
seriousness					

OS MAP: 25
GR: 203394
DISTANCE: 14 miles (22km)
ASCENT: 970m (3,200ft)
TIME: 7½ hours

ASSESSMENT: an easy and enjoyable ascent enhanced by a good lochside approach path, dramatic corries and beautiful surroundings.

NB access restrictions at Struy Bridge limit the time available for the walk.

SEASONAL NOTES: normally no technical difficulties in winter, but care is required on the steep slopes leading up to and down from the summit plateau. The corries are at their finest in winter, but beware corniced corrie rims and ice on the windswept slopes above them.

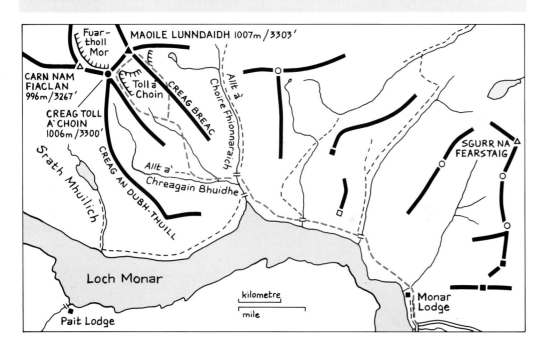

Maoile Lunndaidh's name (meaning Bare Hill of the Boggy Place) and flat plateau summit do not immediately single it out as a prime objective in a region replete with fine hills, but its deeply-cut corries and beautiful approach walk combine Cairngorm grandeur with Western Highland ambience to produce a pleasant and rewarding route. The finest approach to the mountain is from the east via beautifully wooded Glen Strathfarrar, although this must be accomplished against the clock owing to access restrictions at Struy Bridge; a key for the locked gate at the entrance to the glen can be obtained from the cottage beside the gate (phone Struy 260 to check times beforehand).

Begin at Loch Monar dam at the end of the public road and walk along the private road that continues along the lochside to Monar Lodge. Immediately you round a corner to be confronted by what Iain Thomson described in his book *Isolation Shepherd* as 'perhaps the most breath catching shift of scenery in the north'. The view suddenly opens up over the blue waters of Loch Monar to Maoile Lunndaidh's huge Toll a' Choin corrie and its curving plateau summit high in the sky.

From Monar Lodge, continue along the excellent lochside path for 3 miles (5km) to the Allt a' Choire Fhionnaraich, then turn right to follow a path up the near riverbank. At the confluence with the Allt a' Chreagain Bhuidhe after a few hundred metres, cross the river (bridge 100 metres upstream) and take yet another path that climbs beside this stream. After a further ½ mile (1km) the path climbs away from the stream to a fork. Follow the right branch up onto the moor and into the mouth of the deep trench of Toll a' Choin.

Climb broken slopes left of the Toll to gain Maoile Lunndaidh's summit plateau and follow the plateau rim round to Creag Toll a' Choin on the narrow neck of ground between Toll a' Choin and Fuar-tholl Mor, another deep trench that has been gouged out of the far side of the mountain. This is a fine spot, especially in winter, when both corrie rims may be spectacularly corniced. The true summit of Maoile Lunndaidh lies a further ½ mile (1km) away to the north-east across a shallow dip and is difficult to locate on the featureless plateau in mist.

To complete a circuit of Toll a' Choin, descend Maoile Lunndaidh's south-east shoulder, which narrows pleasantly between the Toll and yet another huge corrie to the east. The ridge leads out to the outlying top of Creag Breac, but the easiest way down is to leave the ridge once you are beyond the crags of Toll a' Choin and descend easy ground to rejoin the approach path.

Winter light on the summit plateau of Maoile Lunndaidh.

	1	2	3	4	5
grade					
terrain					
navigation					
seriousness					

OS MAP: 25
GR: 283386
DISTANCE: 15 miles (24km)
ASCENT: 1,550m (5,100ft)
TIME: 8½ hours

ASSESSMENT: a spacious, sweeping ridge walk linking four Munros and two Tops.
NB access restrictions at Struy Bridge limit the time available for the walk.

SEASONAL NOTES: most of the route remains straight-forward in winter, but the steep summit slopes of Sgurr a' Choire Ghlais may give problems, and the descent from Sgurr na Fearstaig can be awkward when the path is obliterated by snow. If time is short, the southern ridges of Sgurr a' Choire Ghlais and Creag Ghorm a' Bhealaich provide easy routes back down to the glen.

The traverse of the six 914m (3,000ft) peaks that border the north side of upper Glen Strathfarrar makes a fine ridge walk, but one that must be accomplished against the clock, owing to access restrictions at Struy Bridge (see Route 26). Begin in Glen Strathfarrar a few hundred metres east of the bridge over the Allt Coire Mhuillidh and take the Land Rover track that becomes a path up into Coire Mhuillidh, an open, heathery corrie backed by three of the route's four Munros. The path continues for a while beside the burn coming down from the bealach between Sgurr na Ruaidhe and Garbh-charn, and then easy grass slopes lead directly to the rounded summit of Sgurr na Ruaidhe.

The other peaks can now be picked off one by one. A swathe of beautifully springy turf sweeps down to the Bealach nam Brogan and up to the bouldery summit of Carn nan Gobhar. The turf then returns to take you down to a deeper bealach and up the steeper slopes of Sgurr a' Choire Ghlais, the reigning peak of the group, whose small summit plateau boasts a trig. pillar and two large cairns. The ridge now narrows around some rugged north-ern corries as it continues over the remaining three closely grouped peaks, whose interven-ing bealachs are relatively shallow and easily crossed (which is why only the central summit is a Munro). The view opens up westwards to reveal a host of peaks crowding the remote shores of Loch Monar.

From the summit of Sgurr a' Choire Ghlais, another awkward boulderfield leads down to

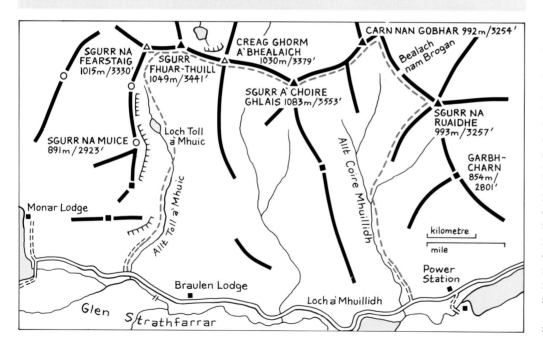

easier slopes and the next bealach, beyond which the going becomes rockier as you climb to the summit of Creag Ghorm a' Bhealaich, perched at the edge of the northern crags and perhaps the finest summit of the whole group. The turf then makes a welcome return as the ridge sweeps onward around the next corrie, which is completely filled by a large lochan, to Sgurr Fhuar-thuill, and then a ten minute stroll leads out to the last top – Sgurr na Fearstaig. Note the cairn on the ridge just before the top, which marks the start of the descent path.

At Sgurr na Fearstaig the ridge turns left over Sgurr na Muice, and this would make an obvious continuation were it not for the excellent descent path, which the author has never been able to resist. It descends past Loch Toll a' Mhuic, whose sandy beach lies at the foot of Sgurr na Muice's craggy east face and is worth a short detour on a hot day. The path eventually becomes a Land Rover track that reaches the roadside 3½ miles (6km) west of your starting point.

Sgurr a' Choire Ghlais from Sgurr Ruaidhe.

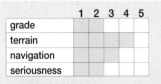

	1	2	3	4	5
grade					
terrain					
navigation					
seriousness					

OS MAP: 24
GR: 834423
DISTANCE: 8 miles (13km)
ASCENT: 940m (3,100ft)
TIME: 6½ hours

ASSESSMENT: a circuit that explores the hidden recesses of a quartet of spectacular corries gouged out of the Applecross Mountains.

SEASONAL NOTES: the corries are magnificent in winter, but the exit from Coire an Fhamhair becomes a steep snow slope that may be corniced and is no place for non-climbers.

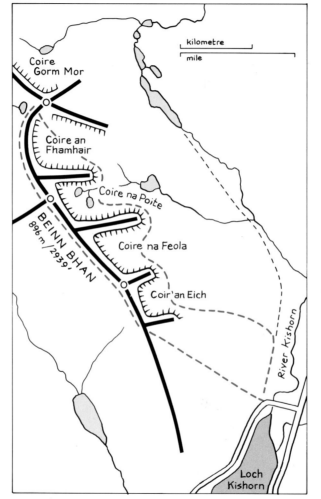

On the coast of Wester Ross a rough barrier of old, red sandstone mountains guards the ancient sanctuary founded on the Applecross peninsula by St. Maelrubha in 673. The highest and most spectacular of the mountains is Beinn Bhan, whose four huge, glacially gouged corries make a fascinating and unusual mountain route.

Begin at the bridge over the Kishorn River on the minor road that leaves the A896 at Tornapress. A path heads north low down on the moor beneath the corries. Follow it until the first corrie, Coir' an Eich (Horse Corrie), comes into view, then strike directly up the rough tangle of rising moor into the mouth of this shallowest of the four corries. Traverse into Coire na Feola (Flesh Corrie) and then around a more pronounced spur into Coire na Poite (Cauldron Corrie). On rounding this spur it is necessary to lose a little height in order to avoid steep broken slopes around the corner, and you may even prefer to make the slight detour down to Lochan Coire na Poite, with its sandy beaches and superb views of the corries.

Climb past waterfalls, up two tiers and over a rock lip to gain inner Coire na Poite, where two hidden lochans lie at the foot of the dramatic 350m (1,200ft) corrie headwall. When snow lies on the terraced ledges of the headwall, this impressive amphitheatre would not look out of place in the Canadian Rockies.

Return to the first tier and contour around the foot of an impressive buttress into the deepest of the four corries, Coire an Fhamhair

(Giant's Corrie), whose left-hand wall is one of the steepest in Scotland. Cross the corrie's grassy flats and climb the steep grass slope in the far right-hand corner to gain the summit plateau of Beinn Bhan. Before turning left to follow the plateau rim to the summit, take a ten minute stroll to the right to the edge of Coire Gorm Mor (Big Green Corrie), for the view over the cliff edge of this hidden fifth corrie to the mountains of Torridon.

On the walk around the plateau rim, spacious views across the Inner Sound to the Cuillin of Skye compete for the attention with the more dramatic views down into the corries. The summit of the mountain lies at the head of Coire na Poite. Continuing beyond, the plateau becomes a narrow ridge on the far side of Coire na Feola, but there is no difficulty and a good path. There is a short rise to the point at the top of the spur between Coire na Feola and Coir' an Eich, and once past Coir' an Eich the route goes directly down the mountainside to your starting point.

Above Coire na Poite and Coire an Fhamhair.

65

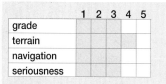

	1	2	3	4	5
grade					
terrain					
navigation					
seriousness					

OS MAP: 24/25
GR: 887541
DISTANCE: 8 miles (13km)
ASCENT: 1,110m (3,650ft)
TIME: 6½ hours

ASSESSMENT: an ascent of a steep buttress well off the beaten track, with some fine situations and some breathtaking coastal views.

SEASONAL NOTES: under snow the eastern buttress may become a steep snow and ice climb; when there is snow on the mountain, non-climbers should stick to an ascent via the Coire Roill descent route described.

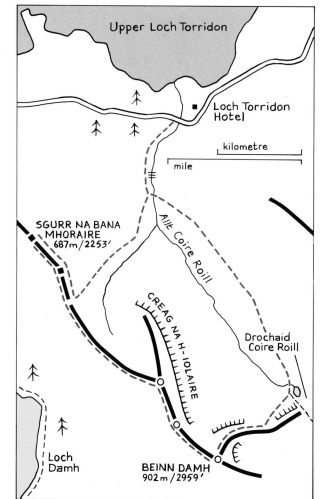

The bold, craggy peaks of the wild Coulin deer forest contain many hidden haunts to tempt the adventurous hillwalker. The three Munros in the area are described in Routes 27 and 28 in *50 Best Routes*, but to the west of these rises another fine mountain that, were it not just under Munro height, would attract much more attention – Beinn Damh. From the west, Beinn Damh's 2 mile (3km) long western wall is an arresting sight, especially the curious Stirrup Mark immediately beneath the summit. Yet the mountain presents an even more dramatic aspect to the east, where a good stalkers' path gives access to the remote north-east spur, which can be climbed directly to the summit.

Begin at the bridge over the Allt Coire Roill 5½ miles (9km) east of Shieldaig on the A896. Seventy metres west of the bridge, a path goes through a gate and climbs pleasantly through woods, among rhododendron bushes and past a high waterfall into Coire Roill. Above the trees the path forks. The right branch will be the route of descent; take the left branch, which crosses the river 200m further on and climbs beneath the impressive cliff face of Creag na h-Iolaire to the Drochaid Coire Roill, the bealach between Beinn Damh and Sgurr na h-Eaglaise.

Leave the path at the lochan on the bealach and cut right beneath a rocky knoll to the foot of the steep east buttress. The next buttress further along on the left looks more interesting but flatters to deceive; its steep heather slopes are best left to mountain goats. Climb the east

buttress directly; it rises steeply in a fine situation and, after levelling off, ends with a short and very easy scramble up Beinn Damh's summit rock tower.

From the summit, follow the bouldery main ridge northwards across a lower top to the stony summit of a second, from where the view back to the final section of the east buttress looks satisfyingly spectacular. The ridge then bears left and descends steeply to the saddle below Sgurr na Bana Mhoraire. This most northern top on the ridge appears distant, but the mesmerising view it affords over Loch Torridon and out to sea is ample recompense for its ascent. There can be few more pleasant spots to rest after the rigours of the ascent than this flat, grassy eyrie, whose Gaelic name (meaning Peak of the Lady) derives from the

Looking southwards along the summit ridge of Beinn Damh towards the summit.

legend of a Lady who was placed there by a cruel Lord and fed with shellfish (whose shells can still be seen!). To descend, return to the saddle and descend left into Coire Roill to pick up the path, mentioned above, that rejoins the outward route.

	1	2	3	4	5
grade					
terrain					
navigation					
seriousness					

OS MAP: 19/25
GR: 025611
DISTANCE: 6 miles (10km)
ASCENT: 950m (3,100ft)
TIME: 5½ hours

ASSESSMENT: a corrie skyline circuit that includes a spectacular scramble over the fearsome Black Carls of Beinn Eighe, with a path that avoids any insurmountable difficulties if necessary.

SEASONAL NOTES: in winter the traverse of the Black Carls is for experienced winter climbers only and, if the path around them is obliterated by snow, this section of the Beinn Eighe ridge is best avoided by walkers.

'I was presently aware of an obstacle that, looming through the cloud, wore an exceedingly forbidding appearance. It was a pinnacle on the top of my ridge – one of the three, known as the Black Regiment, which you can see from the valley. I learned afterwards that those pinnacles are not as bad as they look; they certainly could not be as formidable as that half-seen menace suggested.'

W. KERSLEY HOLMES
(Tramping Scottish Hills, 1946)

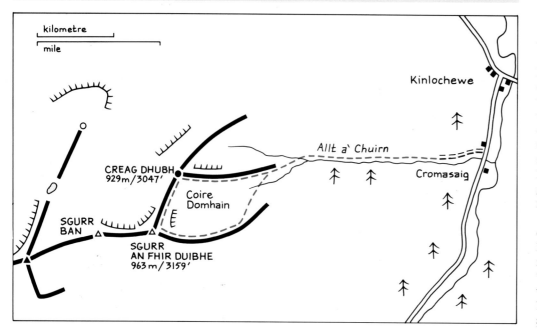

The 3 mile (5km) long main ridge of Beinn Eighe dominates the landscape west of Kinlochewe. Route 31 in *50 Best Routes* explores the magnificent western reaches of the mountain, but the most exciting section on the main ridge is undoubtedly its far eastern end, where the pinnacles known as the Black Carls (Black Men) of Sgurr an Fhir Duibhe await the intrepid ridge wanderer. Those who have undertaken the western route and already glimpsed this part of the ridge will need no further incentive.

From Kinlochewe, the view of Beinn Eighe's quartzite eastern heights brings to mind Principal Shairp's evocative description of the mountain in his poem on Glen Torridon: 'magnificent alp blanched bare and bald and white'. Above a skirt of grass and scree the Black Carls etch the skyline of Coire Domhain and hold out an irresistible challenge. The route described here follows the corrie skyline.

Begin beside the house 150 metres north of the bridge over the Allt a' Chuirn, ½ mile (1km) south of Kinlochewe on the A896 Torridon road. Take the rough track that continues as a path up the wooded left bank (right side) of the river into Coire Domhain. From here, climb the stony ridge that bounds the corrie on the right (north) to gain the skyline and reach Creag Dhubh, Beinn Eighe's most easterly 914m (3,000ft) top, then follow the main ridge south-westwards over another rise to reach the Black Carls.

Do not be put off by the fearsome appearance and reputation of the Black Carls, for they provide a sporting scramble on good holds. A path weaves among them, and indeed some of them are best bypassed, depending on your scrambling ability, but many can be taken direct. The only real problem is the final 10m (30ft) wall up to the summit slopes of Sgurr an Fhir Duibhe, but this too provides excellent holds for ascent. Alternatively, climb a gully on the left, or avoid all difficulties by a path that circumvents the entire crag further left.

Complete the round of Coire Domhain by descending Sgurr an Fhir Duibhe's easy east ridge, which is the corrie's southern bounding rim. When the ridge levels off, drop down into the corrie to pick up the path back to Cromasaig.

The Black Carls of Sgurr an Fhir Duibhe, Beinn Eighe.

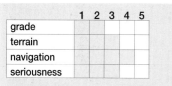

	1	2	3	4	5
grade					
terrain					
navigation					
seriousness					

OS MAP: 19
GR: 033624
DISTANCE: 12 miles (19km)
ASCENT: 1,160m (3,800ft)
TIME: 8 hours

ASSESSMENT: a beautiful approach and an interesting horseshoe ridge walk, offering great views, on the impressive looking Spear.

SEASONAL NOTES: in winter steep snow slopes may be encountered in several places, especially on the descent from the summit and from Sgurr Dubh. Under snow the ridge between Sgurr an Tuill Bhain and Slioch's north top makes for a good introduction to narrow winter ridge walking.

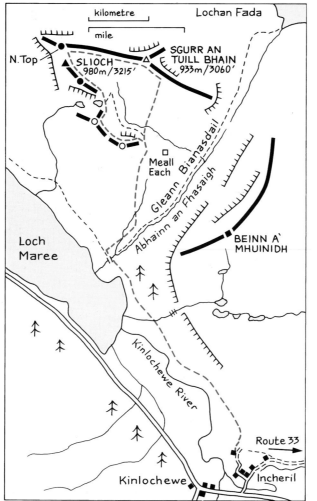

Slioch is a bold, isolated chunk of a mountain that rises directly from the western shore of beautiful Loch Maree and well suits its evocative Gaelic name (meaning The Spear). Its distinctive shape derives from its two-tiered geological structure; its base is a plinth of ice-scoured gneiss, while its summit is a great pyramid of Torridonian sandstone guarded by cliffs on three sides. The only easy access is from the south, where the sandstone has been hollowed by Coire Tuill Bhain.

The route begins in Incheril east of Kinlochewe, at the end of the first road on the left after leaving the A832. Walk past the farmhouse and keep left on a track that becomes a path along the beautifully wooded right bank of the Kinlochewe River, beneath the cliffs of Beinn a' Mhuinidh and its 100m (300ft) waterfall. After 3 miles (5 km) cross the Abhainn an Fhasaigh (bridge) and take the path up deep-cut Gleann Bianasdail. Keep left at a cairned fork after a couple of hundred metres to climb onto the moor, then keep left again at another cairned fork further along to follow a well-trodden path that climbs steeply up a shallow depression, around the foot of Sgurr Dubh and into the flat bowl of Coire Tuill Bhain.

Leave the path to cross the corrie and climb grassy slopes littered with rocks to the south-east ridge and summit of Sgurr an Tuill Bhain on the corrie's eastern rim. The magnificent view northwards from here across The Great Wilderness will make you impatient to explore its remote peaks (Routes 32 and 33). The

horseshoe ridge walk around the corrie begins here with a descent to a dip, and then the ridge narrows pleasantly, though without difficulty, as it rises and broadens to Slioch's north top, perched above the cliffs of the impressive north-west face. Scramblers may wish to explore the continuing north-west spur for a more intimate appraisal of the rock scenery. The main summit of Slioch lies just a further five minutes away around the cliff top.

The path back along the corrie's western rim may be difficult to locate in mist because of stony ground. It goes south-eastwards across a low rise and then trends further eastwards to find the top of a steep stony spur, left of cliffs; this gives access to the left-hand edge of the saddle below, with its two lochans. From the saddle the main path descends to the corrie,

Slioch from Lochan Fada.

but it is instead worth continuing around the ridge to Sgurr Dubh, the last nail in the horse-shoe and an eyrie above the southern reaches of Loch Maree. From Sgurr Dubh, descend steep grass slopes in the direction of Meall Each to regain the outward path at the top of the shallow depression.

Route 32: A' MHAIGHDEAN • The Northern Highlands

	1	2	3	4	5
grade					
terrain					
navigation					
seriousness					

OS MAP: 19
GR: 859807
DISTANCE: 27 miles (43km)
ASCENT: 1,110m (3,650ft)
TIME: 13 hours

Carnmore approach (each way):
10 miles (16km), **out** 260m
(850ft) **back** 80m (250ft), 4 hrs
Ascent from Carnmore:
7 miles (11km), 770m (2,550ft),
5 hrs

ASSESSMENT: a stirring trek
and scramble to the top of
Britain's most remote peak.

SEASONAL NOTES: a unique
winter expedition, impossible to
undertake from any roadside in a
single day. The north-west ridge
is a difficult proposition under
snow and, even on an ascent by
the descent route described,
steep snow slopes near the
summit may cause problems.

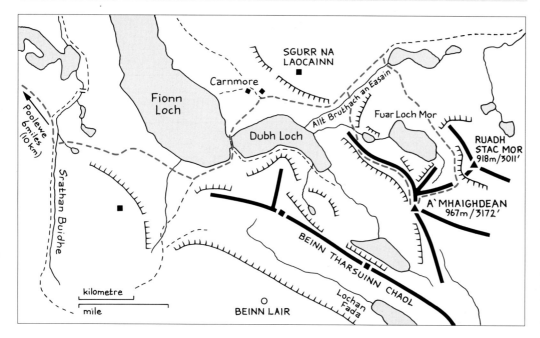

East of Slioch lies the Great Wilderness, a vast stretch of wild land whose mountains are remote and serious undertakings. The most elusive and prized of all is the shapely peak of A' Mhaighdean, whose ascent in a single day requires fitness and determination.

The easiest approach starts in Poolewe; park opposite the church 100 metres along the minor road on the east bank of the River Ewe. From here it is 10 miles (16km) to Carnmore at the foot of the mountain. A road/track covers the first 4 miles (6½km) and a mountain bike can be used to shorten the approach.

At the edge of the wood beyond Kernsary, fork right into the wood and leave the track at a cairned left-hand bend for a tiresomely boggy path that follows the Allt na Creige up onto the crest of the moor beneath the crags of Beinn Airigh Charr. Once over the crest the going improves and soon an excellent stalkers' path is joined (GR 940767; note the junction for the return journey). A short-cut avoids the long detour shown on the map across the Srathan Buidhe, and then the path heads down to the causeway between the Fionn (White) loch and the Dubh (Black) Loch to reach Carnmore Lodge and bothy, situated in as wild a spot as you could wish for. **NB** the bothy is not in a habitable state at the time of writing.

Continue along the path as it climbs beneath the cliffs of Sgurr na Laocainn to the gorge of the Allt Bruthach an Easain. Leave it to cross the burn at the head of the gorge and traverse across the hillside to reach A' Mhaighdean's stepped north-west ridge, which rises amid wonderfully rugged and complex terrain. A developing path weaves upwards among the many outcrops, requiring occasional handwork and one short scramble up an easy rock step. Higher up, the ridge erupts into insurmountable rock towers, but the path finds a way around them with unexpected ease and soon deposits you at the well-won summit.

To descend, go down steep grass slopes to the bealach between A' Mhaighdean and its neighbouring Munro Ruadh Stac Mor. The ascent of Ruadh Stac Mor would add only 170m (560ft) and 1 hour to the route, but tackling the stone shoots that thread through a band of broken sandstone crags to the stony summit slopes above would take great determination (descent can be made at a break in the crags further along). From the bealach, a path descends above Fuar Loch Mor onto Ruadh Stac Mor's north-west shoulder, from where a good stalkers' path returns you to the gorge of the Allt Bruthach an Easain to complete the circle. All that remains now is the short stroll back to Poolewe.

A' Mhaighdean and Ruadh Stac Mor from Lochan Fada.

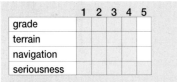

	1	2	3	4	5
grade					
terrain					
navigation					
seriousness					

OS MAP: 19
GR: 036622
DISTANCE: 20 miles (32km)
ASCENT: 1,400m (4,600ft)
TIME: 11hours

Lochan Fada approach (each way):
  7 miles (11km), **out** via Gleann na
  Muice 300m (1,000ft) **back** via
  Gleann Bianasdail 80m (250ft),
  3 hours.
Ascent from Lochan Fada:
  6 miles (10km), 1,020m (3,350ft),
  5½ hours.

ASSESSMENT: a long, wild and
magnificent traverse across narrow,
rocky ridges at the heart of The Great
Wilderness.

SEASONAL NOTES: the complete
route is a lengthy trip for a short
winter's day. Steep snow slopes
abound and the pinnacles of Sgurr
Dubh are a serious proposition under
snow; the south ridge of Meall Garbh
provides an easier descent route.

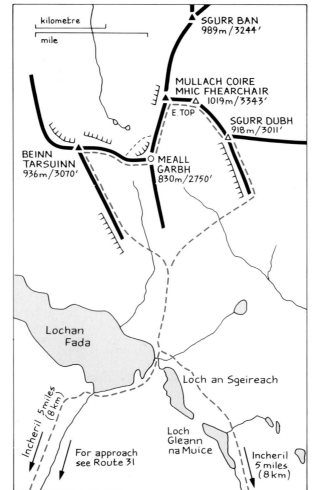

Mullach Coire Mhic Fhearchair is the highest mountain in The Great Wilderness and its ascent in a single day is, fittingly, a considerable and superb expedition. The route begins at Incheril near Kinlochewe, as for Slioch (see Route 31). Take the Land Rover track that goes to the Heights of Kinlochewe and forks left up Gleann na Muice, then continue along an excellent path to the shores of remote and beautiful Lochan Fada.

Follow the right bank (left side) of the small stream that drains into the end of the loch to find a cairned route, with developing path, that takes the easiest line up to the low point on the skyline. From here, go left to gain the top of crags overlooking Lochan Fada and cross broken rock pavement to the grassy summit slopes of Beinn Tarsuinn.

The summit cairn is perched at the edge of the vertiginous northern corrie and gives superb views of the mountains at the heart of the Wilderness. Superfit scramblers should take time out to explore the western corrie rim, whose crest of sandstone blocks gives lovely easy scrambling in a fine situation.

Eastwards from Beinn Tarsuinn grassy slopes lead down to a bealach, beyond which the way to Mullach Coire Mhic Fhearchair is barred by the craggy lump of Meall Garbh; this can be either climbed over or contoured around on the understandably well-worn traverse path. A steep ascent then gains the awkward, broken quartzite summit cap of Mullach Coire Mhic Fhearchair, where you will undoubtedly put hand to rock more times than intended. Turning eastwards once more, easier going leads across a dip to the Mullach's east top, and then the ridge narrows to provide wonderful ridge walking. Across the next dip things become even more exciting as the ridge erupts into a series of spectacular and complex pinnacles rising to Sgurr Dubh. The scrambling is mostly easy but everywhere sensational, and there are some places where, like the author, you may wish to bail out onto the exposed little path that weaves among the pinnacles.

From the summit, continue down easier slopes to a levelling and then down a further craggy steepening to outflank cliffs and gain the corrie below. Cross the corrie to regain the low point on the skyline on the far side and then keep right of a small stream to find the cairned route down to Lochan Fada.

To complete a memorable circuit, walk round the loch end and return to Incheril via the path down Gleann Bianasdail and across the grassy flats beside the Kinlochewe River; this is a rougher but more scenic route than the Gleann na Muice approach (see Route 31).

Mullach Coire Mhic Fhearchair from Beinn Tarsuinn.

	1	2	3	4	5
grade					
terrain					
navigation					
seriousness					

OS MAP: 20
GR: 238759
DISTANCE: 10½ miles (17km)
ASCENT: 1,190m (3,900ft)
TIME: 7½ hours

ASSESSMENT: a spacious walk over three Munros that form part of the best easy high-level ridge walk in the Northern Highlands. The route can easily be extended to include more Munros.

SEASONAL NOTES: a magnificent winter tramp that can be curtailed or extended according to time and inclination. Steep snow may be encountered on the ascent of Sgurr Mor, and snow on the corrie headwall beneath the Meall a' Chrasgaidh bealach may cause unexpected problems until late in the year.

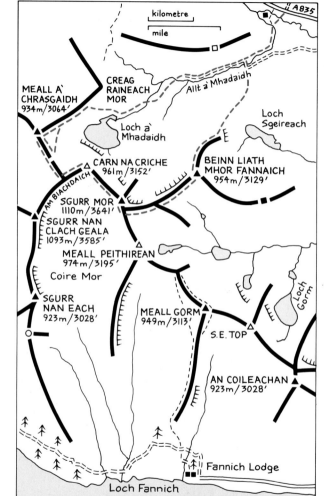

A compact group of nine Munros lying south of Braemore Junction on the A835 Dingwall–Ullapool road, the Fannichs are wild, windswept hills that provide spacious walking reminiscent of the Mamores. The heart of the range is the desolate mountain fastness of Loch Fannich and Coire Mor, around which the main spine of the Fannichs forms a huge crescent. A Land Rover track runs to the lochside, but a current unenlightened access policy prohibits its public use and makes some Fannichs difficult to reach. The route described here takes in the three central peaks, including the highest, and gives the option of adding on others.

Begin at a parking space on the north side of the A835, 2½ miles (4km) east of Braemore Junction and a couple of hundred metres east of a small building on the south side of the road. A developing path crosses the moor to join a good stalkers' path at a bridge over the Allt a' Mhadaidh. This in turn joins a Land Rover track from Loch Droma. Follow the track and the stalkers' path that continues from its end to Loch a' Mhadaidh, one of the Fannichs' many fine, wild lochans. From here, aim right to gain the top of Creag Raineach Mor and another path that comes up from Braemore Junction. This contours left onto the bealach south of Meall a' Chrasgaidh to avoid steep ground; alternatively the broken craggy spur to its right gives an easy scramble directly to the summit.

From the summit gentle slopes lead pleasantly across a broad bealach and the rich pastures of Am Biachdaich to the edge of Coire Mor and the summit of Carn na Criche. Sgurr nan Clach Geala and Sgurr nan Each, the two Munros on the west side of Coire Mor, can be added to the route here. Beyond Carn na Criche a shallow bealach leads to a relentless 220m (720ft) ascent up the steep summit cone of Sgurr Mor, the reigning peak of the group.

The main ridge sweeps temptingly onwards across Meall nan Peithirean and Meall Gorm to An Coileachan and the edge of the magnificent Garbh Choire Mor, perhaps the Fannichs' finest feature. The return route from Sgurr Mor soon leaves this ridge to bear eastwards across a saddle between two corries to Beinn Liath Mhor Fannaich. There is an intermittent good path, but unfortunately this path bypasses the summit boulderfield. The descent back to the Allt a' Mhadaidh is quite rough; follow the ridge as it trends north then north-east and, keeping left of crags, go straight off the end, down the shoulder and across the moor to rejoin the Land Rover track at the bridge where it crosses the river.

Sgurr Mor from Meall a' Chrasgaidh.

	1	2	3	4	5
grade					
terrain					
navigation					
seriousness					

OS MAP: 20
GR: 412673
DISTANCE: 8 miles (13km)
ASCENT: 940m (3,100ft)
TIME: 5 hours

ASSESSMENT: a straight-forward ascent leads to a pleasant stroll across an ecologically unique mountain summit.

SEASONAL NOTES: in normal winter conditions this mountain provides a good introduction to winter walking (and ski-mountaineering). The muted golden colours of the summit moss are at their most beautiful in autumn.

The flat summit skyline and featureless western slopes of Ben Wyvis will not immediately catch the eye of the connoisseur or excite the imagination in the same way as the shapely peaks of the west. The only physical features of any note on the mountain are two great corries, Coire Mor and Coire na Feola, which have been gouged out of the hidden eastern side of the mountain. Yet the mountain's vast isolated bulk is eventually impossible to ignore. Wyvis dominates Easter Ross to such an extent that it demands to be climbed, and those who do so will find at its summit extensive views and an ecologically unique plateau that makes the effort well worthwhile.

It is a walker's mountain par excellence, with seven tops over 914m (3,000ft) and a straightforward route to the summit from the west, normally without undue difficulty even under the snow that lies late into the year.

Begin at the bridge over the Allt a' Bhealaich Mhoir, amid extensive forestry plantations, near Garbat on the A835 Dingwall–Ullapool road (parking spaces 100 metres south along the road). Take the path, signposted Ben Wyvis Footpath, that climbs the clearing between the river and the forest fence, then bear left above the forest to climb the steepening west ridge of An Cabar, the southernmost top of the Wyvis group.

Here begins the unique Glas Leathad Mor, a soft carpet of moss that extends for 1½ miles (2km) along the roof of the mountain to the summit, giving wonderful walking on some of the most unusual mountain terrain in Scotland.

Under the right atmospheric conditions, with mist clinging to the glen or shafts of light piercing brooding clouds over the hills to the west, many a more shapely peak is easily forgotten.

From the summit the mountain's northerly tops can be visited by those who wish to extend the day. It is possible to make a circuit back to Garbat across the boggy moorland and through the labyrinthine forest, but this is likely to lead to aggravation rather than the roadside, and for once it is perhaps best to descend via the ascent route.

Historical note: Ben Wyvis's late-lying snow made it possible for the MacKenzie Earls of Cromarty to rent their land from the Crown on condition that they could produce a snowball at any time of year.

Ecological note: there are recurrent proposals for a downhill ski development on Ben Wyvis, which includes the building of a railway from Strathpeffer on to the slopes of the mountain itself and brings developers into conflict with conservationists. Ben Wyvis has been designated a National Nature Reserve and a Site of Special Scientific Interest, but only time will tell who wins the battle for its long-term future.

An Cabar from above the forest.

	1	2	3	4	5
grade					
terrain					
navigation					
seriousness					

OS MAP: 20
GR: 267750
DISTANCE: 11 miles (17km)
ASCENT: 1,180m (3,850ft)
TIME: 7½ hours

ASSESSMENT: a complex approach route leads to a skyline circuit of a majestic corrie in rough, lonely country.

SEASONAL NOTES: in winter the ascent to and traverse of Cona' Mheall's south-east ridge are not for beginners; in normal winter conditions an easier ascent/descent route is via the head of Coire Ghranda, although steep snow may be encountered here. Routefinding on the summit dome of Beinn Dearg is difficult in adverse weather, especially so in winter.

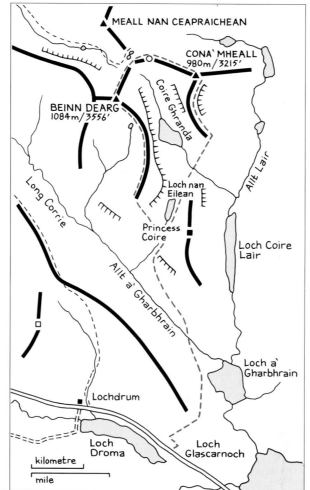

When driving north across the Dirrie More on the A835 to Ullapool, the craggy summits of Beinn Dearg and Cona' Mheall can be seen rising over the wild moorland north of Loch Glascarnoch. They are an irresistible attraction, especially as between the two lies the grossly misnamed Coire Ghranda (Ugly Corrie), yet another of those magnificent and remote hidden corries for which the Northern Highlands are famous. A circuit of the corrie skyline, which takes in the two summits, provides a problematical and engrossing route in lonely country.

The easiest approach route makes use of an old path that is no longer marked on the OS map. Begin at the lay-by at the south-east end of Loch Droma and go straight up the hillside for about 50m to meet a path along an old drove road, marked by a cairned boulder. Go left along the path for a few hundred metres, then leave it just before another cairned boulder for an overgrown path that cuts back right up the hillside, improving with height. This path contours around the hillside to end at the ruins of an old shieling near Loch a' Gharbhrain.

Follow the Allt a' Gharbhrain up into the boggy Long Corrie, crossing the river wherever practicable (this is notoriously difficult to do dryshod and may be impossible in spate). Once across, aim diagonally up the hillside into the rough heathery trough of the Princess Corrie. Here the serrated skyline of Cona' Mheall is seen for the first time, mirrored in

Loch nan Eilean. Continue through the corrie, descend slightly across the entrance to Coire Ghranda and pick a steep route up among rock outcrops to Cona' Mheall's south-east ridge, from where Coire Ghranda's lochan and encircling 450m (1,500ft) cliffs look spectacular.

The ridge is narrow and slabby, but of little difficulty unless the rock is wet and greasy, when care is required. Short scrambles are required to descend to a level section of ridge and re-ascend to the high point of the ridge, beyond which a short dip leads to gentle boulder slopes curving right to the summit. The route to Beinn Dearg goes west around the head of Coire Ghranda, contouring to lochans on the Bealach Coire Ghranda at the foot of Beinn Dearg's rough north-east slopes. From here, climb directly to Beinn Dearg's summit dome, following the line of a dry stone wall most of the way.

The most interesting descent route follows the ridge that forms the western rim of Coire Ghranda (difficult to locate in mist). Hold to the ridge when it crosses a saddle and surmounts a rise; then bear right above the crags bordering the Princess Corrie to descend to the corrie entrance and rejoin the route of ascent.

Coire Ghranda from the Bealach Coire Ghranda.

Route 37: SEANA BHRAIGH • THE NORTHERN HIGHLANDS

	1	2	3	4	5
grade					
terrain					
navigation					
seriousness					

OS MAP: 20
GR: 327953
DISTANCE: 13½ miles (21km)
ASCENT: 920m (3,000ft)
TIME: 8 hours

Approach (each way):
  4 miles (6km), **out** 110m (350ft),
  1½ hours
Ascent:
  5½ miles (9km), 810m (2,650ft),
  5 hours.

ASSESSMENT: a scramble around one of the Northern Highlands' great corries on a peak well off the beaten track. **NB** the route can be done in either direction; the anti-clockwise route described involves more descent on rock but tackles the most exposed scrambling on ascent.

SEASONAL NOTES: in winter be prepared for steep snow slopes near the summit. The traverse of An Sgurr under snow is a major expedition of Alpine character.

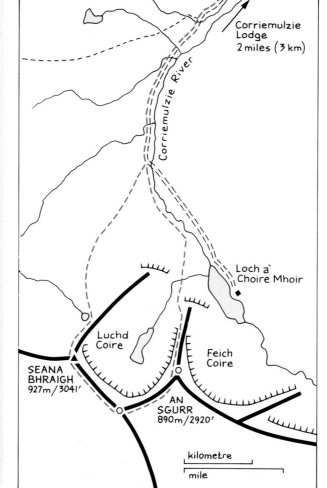

From Beinn Dearg to the south, Seana Bhraigh appears as a featureless plateau hardly worthy of investigation, but from the north it shows its true colours as a mountain of dramatic features. Especially notable is the pointed spur of An Sgurr, which forms the eastern boundary of the great Luchd Coire, whose cliffs rise 400m (1,300ft) from the lochan cupped in its depths. From Strathmulzie a circuit of Luchd Coire combines an easy ascent with an exciting scramble over An Sgurr.

The route begins near Corriemulzie Lodge, reached by a 6 mile (10km) long track from Oykel Bridge on the A867; it is normally possible to drive up and park at the shed at the foot of the hill before the lodge. Walk (or mountain bike) along the rough track for a further 4 miles (6km), until it crosses the river, then head up grassy slopes directly for the summit of Seana Bhraigh. The rim of Luchd Coire is reached at the small lochan just beyond Point 760, and the view from here across the yawning depths of the corrie to the fluted rock buttresses of An Sgurr is very impressive. The summit of Seana Bhraigh is perched at the very edge of the corrie headwall and boasts an extensive view, especially to the north, where a frieze of Sutherland peaks line the horizon.

A broad plateau-like ridge leads onwards around the corrie rim, crossing a saddle to another top and then a deeper saddle to the summit arête of An Sgurr. The excitement begins when you reach a gap that must be crossed just before the summit. Ledges on the left enable the sharp ridgecrest to be avoided at first, but soon you reach an unavoidable, steep 3m wall that must be descended. After pause for thought, you will find it goes easily enough, especially facing outwards. The next rocky step is again avoided on the left by a ledge that deposits you in the gap. The ascent to the summit is not as bad as it first looks but is quite exposed; it can be avoided by grass slopes on the right if necessary.

From the summit one more steep but easy descent ends the main scramble and leads to a point from where the north-west ridge drops steeply away beneath your feet. The descent of the ridge is nowhere difficult, but there is plenty of handwork still to come and care is required (do not let your rucksack push you away from the rock). At the top of the craggy lower buttress, go left down steep grass slopes, cross the mouth of Luchd Coire, and follow the banks of the Corriemulzie River back down to the track and your starting point.

An Sgurr from across Luchd Coire.

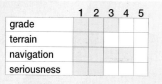

Route 38: BEN HOPE • THE NORTHERN HIGHLANDS

	1	2	3	4	5
grade					
terrain					
navigation					
seriousness					

OS MAP: 9
GR: 462477
DISTANCE: 6 miles (10km)
ASCENT: 910m (3,000ft)
TIME: 5 hours

ASSESSMENT: a route of surprises and panoramic views over the Pentland Firth on Scotland's most northerly and most isolated mainland Munro. **NB** the route is graded 3, but a direct ascent of the rock step on the north ridge is Grade 5.

SEASONAL NOTES: in winter the north ridge is for experienced mountaineers only. The mountain's south-west slopes offer an easier ascent route, but they are steep and require care under snow, especially when iced.

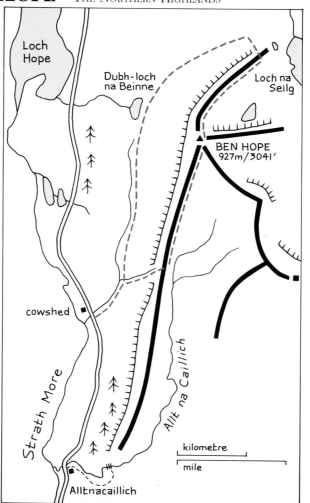

The craggy wedge of Ben Hope stands isolated on the shores of Loch Hope, less than a dozen miles (20km) from the north coast of Scotland, and makes a fitting most northerly Munro. It must have been a stirring sight to the Vikings of old after their hazardous journey across the sea, and it is the only Munro that they named (Hope is Norse for Bay, referring to nearby Loch Eriboll). Because of its isolation, Ben Hope's summit has an air of spaciousness unequalled on the mainland. Many Munro baggers choose it as the last Munro on their list and ascend it via the normal route up the relentless south-west slopes, but Best Route connoisseurs will spurn this approach for the far more interesting north ridge, with its sensational rock step (avoidable).

The route begins near a cowshed, 2 miles (3km) north of Dun Dornaigil broch on the Road of Desolation in wild Strath More. A path ascends the left bank (right side) of a stream, but leave it when it heads up to a breach in the western cliffs (the normal route and the route of descent). Instead, continue northwards beside the main stream onto the shelf holding Dubh-loch na Beinne, and keep going until a way can be made up onto the north ridge near Loch na Seilg at its far end.

The broad ridge rises to a cairn, beyond which a short dip leads to a spectacular 10m (30ft) section of exposed scrambling on the edge of the west face. Go to the foot of it for the view over the edge, and try it if you have the nerve, otherwise take the not

surprisingly well-worn path up the gully 30m to the left, regaining the ridge above all difficulties. The ridge continues narrowly to the summit dome, from where there are commanding views all around the compass.

Descend via the normal route, following the path down the south-west slopes. The path bears right at a height of 400m (1,300ft) to breach the cliffs and descend beside a stream to regain the route of ascent (care in mist; if in doubt about where to descend, continue southwards, cross the Allt na Caillich and descend a path to Alltnacaillich in Strath More).

Historical note: Strath More is a desolate and lonely area, perhaps reflecting its troubled history. The greatest time of suffering was during the brutal Sutherland Clearances, when in

Ben Hope towers over Loch Hope.

October 1819 100 young men of Strath More and their families were shipped off to Ontario; all were lost at sea in winter storms. Their houses were demolished 'because they showed the devastation where people had lived' and the stones used to lay the foundations of the Road of Desolation.

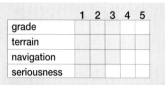

	1	2	3	4	5
grade					
terrain					
navigation					
seriousness					

OS MAP: 10
GR: 584547
DISTANCE: 10½ miles (17km)
ASCENT: 880m (2,900ft)
TIME: 7 hours

ASSESSMENT: an entertaining circuit on a scrambler's playground high above the Pentland Firth.

SEASONAL NOTES: in winter it may be best to avoid the descent of the nose of Sgor a' Chleiridh, otherwise the route is normally of no especial difficulty for those competent on snow, except for iced rocks on summit tors.

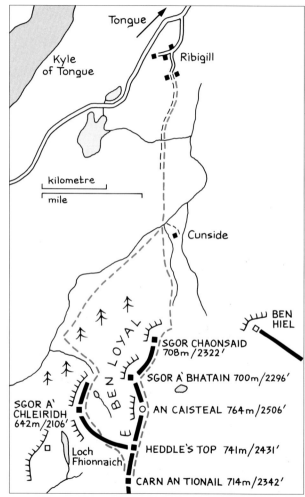

Despite its modest height, Ben Loyal is a true mountain range in miniature that is a distinctive feature of the north coast of Scotland. Its several granite tops, reminiscent of Cairngorm tors, set some enjoyable (optional) bouldering problems for those who like to seek a spot of scrambling, and they also form an attractive skyline frieze that has given rise to the mountain's flattering epithet: 'Queen of the Scottish Peaks'.

The shortest approach to Ben Loyal is from the east beside Loch Loyal, but this is beset by boggy terrain and best avoided. The most aesthetic approach is from the north, where the several tops are seen arrayed across the moor, showing their best profile, and a path enables easy access to the foot of the mountain. The route begins at the start of the private road to Ribigill Farm, 1½ miles (2km) south of Tongue village on the old road around the Kyle of Tongue. Walk to the farm and continue along the farm track that heads south across the moor to Cunside Cottage. Near Cunside, and marked on the OS map, is Uaigh Dhiarmaid (Jeremy's Grave), a chambered cairn that is only one of many prehistoric sites in the area.

The track becomes a path that passes the cottage on the right and climbs the left bank (right side) of the burn coming down from the craggy north face of Sgor Chaonsaid. Climb steep grass and heather left of the face to reach the summit tors, from where the view is as extensive as you would expect from such an isolated mountain.

Ben Loyal's other tops can now be visited one by one. After a short dip comes Sgor a' Bhatain, whose twin tors (The Boats) project slightly west of the main ridge, but which scramblers should be sure to visit. Next is crag-girt An Caisteal, the highest top, and then the grassy summit of Heddle's Top. Finally comes Carn an Tionail, beyond which lower bumps of little interest lead down to the moor.

The entertainment, however, is far from over. From Carn an Tionail, return to the dip before Heddle's Top and contour round to Heddle's Top's broad west ridge. This leads out to the narrow summit of Sgor a' Chleiridh, the sharpest of all Ben Loyal's tops, with an impressive south-west face towering above the sandy beaches of Loch Fhionnaich and sporting excellent rock routes almost 300m (1,000ft) long. With care, continue over the nose of Sgor a' Chleiridh and pick a route down the north-east ridge among outcrops, then follow sheep tracks down the right bank of the burn through fine birch woods to reach the moor. From here make a beeline back across the moor to the Cunside path.

Light and darkness on Sgor a' Chleiridh.

Route 40: BEINN A' GHLO · THE CAIRNGORMS

	1	2	3	4	5
grade					
terrain					
navigation					
seriousness					

OS MAP: 43
GR: 901718
DISTANCE: 14½ miles (23km)
ASCENT: 1,420m (4,650ft)
TIME: 9 hours

ASSESSMENT: a wild tramp along the broad, undulating ridges of the three Munros that form the windswept Mountain of Mist.

SEASONAL NOTES: a classic winter walk but one whose length should not be underestimated. There are normally no technical difficulties, but steep snow may be encountered on occasion and care is required on the often iced ridges as in many places a slip would be very difficult to arrest. If short of time, the route can be curtailed by a descent of the south-west ridge of Braigh Coire Chruinn-bhalgain.

'As we left the wood we came upon such a lovely view – Beinn a' Ghlo straight before us – and under these high hills the River Tilt gushing and winding over stones and slates, and the hills and mountains skirted at the bottom with beautiful trees; the whole lit up by the sun; and the air so pure and fine; but no description can at all do it justice.'

QUEEN VICTORIA describing a drive up Glen Tilt in 1844.

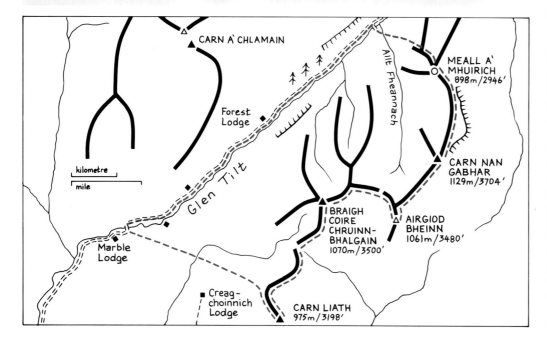

The complex mountain of Beinn a' Ghlo rises out of the bare landscape north-east of Blair Atholl. According to an old sporting legend, its three Munros support no less than nineteen corries, in any one of which a rifle can be fired without being heard in any other, but it is the long, high ridges that are the main attraction for hillwalkers.

The best approach to the mountain is the rough private road along Glen Tilt that begins at Old Bridge of Tilt near Blair Atholl (GR 875663). Permission to drive the 4½ miles (7km) to the start of the route at the bridge just past Marble Lodge can be obtained from Atholl Estates Office in Blair Atholl (tel: 079-681-355). From the bridge, climb diagonally up the hillside to the low ridge on the south side of the glen, then cross windswept moors and negotiate steep heathery slopes to reach the summit of Carn Liath.

The route onwards is a bracing high-level walk along the broad grassy main ridge as it

snakes down to a bealach and sweeps up to the wonderfully named Braigh Coire Chruinn-bhalgain (Upland of the Corrie of the Round Little Blisters). Beyond here a twist right and left leads to a small rise, and then the main ridge turns immediately right (east) again to cross a bealach and climb to the summit ridge of Carn nan Gabhar, Beinn a' Ghlo's highest top. In mist the right turn to the bealach is not obvious, as the ridge line trends northwards along a subsidiary ridge, and note that Beinn a' Ghlo's Gaelic name does not mean Mountain of Mist for nothing. Once on the summit ridge, you might as well bear right to bag the nearby Top of Airgiod Bheinn before returning and continuing out to Carn nan Gabhar. Note in mist that the highest point is about 200m beyond the trig. pillar. The easiest way to

Battling the wind on Carn Liath, with Braigh Coire Chruinn-bhalgain ahead.

regain Glen Tilt is to continue northwards over Meall a' Mhuirich and descend to the bridge over the River Tilt at the foot of the Allt Fheannach (GR 956763). The day ends with a pleasant 4 mile (6km) riverside walk back down the confines of the deep, V-shaped glen.

	1	2	3	4	5
grade					
terrain					
navigation					
seriousness					

OS MAP: 44
GR: 283761
DISTANCE: 9 miles (15km)
ASCENT: 980m (3,200ft)
TIME: 6 hours

ASSESSMENT: a sky-high stroll across a rolling plateau, which is approached by excellent paths through beautiful corries and glens.

SEASONAL NOTES: a normally straightforward winter route, although the steep exit from Corrie Fee may pose problems under snow; those without experience should ascend via the Kilbo Path instead. The broken crags on the left of the corrie hold snow into summer and have long been the haunt of Dundonian climbers seeking winter routes.

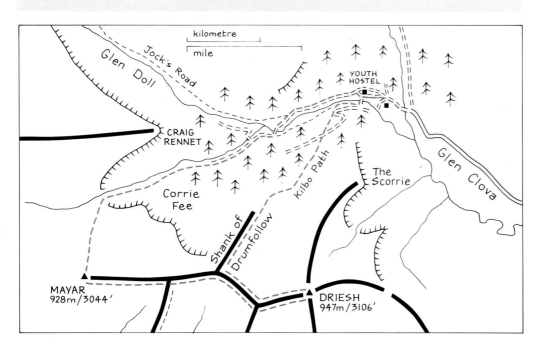

South of Deeside lies the great rolling table-land of the White Mounth. In several places the high moor heaves itself up to the 914m (3,000ft) contour, causing minor excrescences to reach Munro status, and providing miles of high, open country for those who love long, lonely moorland tramps. The major features of interest are the corries and glens that indent the tableland on all sides, and these make for some unexpectedly rewarding hillwalking. One of the finest expeditions in the area is the round of Driesh and Mayar, the two Munros on the southern perimeter of the plateau. The mountains are reached by the B955 road along Glen Clova, a great U-shaped glen, flanked by a succession of hanging corries, that is one of the foremost examples of glacial scenery in Scotland. The scenery is almost Alpine.

Begin at the car park at the road end and take the Land Rover track (Jock's Road) that continues straight on past Acharn along densely wooded Glen Doll. Ignore all side tracks and paths, including that which branches right to carry Jock's Road to Deeside. After 1½ miles (2km) the track crosses the White Water and follows the right bank (left side) of the tumbling Fee Burn up towards Corrie Fee. When the track ends, a path continues to the lip of the corrie at the entrance to Caenlochan National Nature Reserve.

The beautiful corrie, with its green meadows, meandering stream, fine waterfall and encircling crags, is a secret, peaceful and picturesque haven. Follow the path across the

interesting moraines on the flat floor of the corrie and either clamber up beside the waterfall or take the main path further left to exit from the corrie onto the rolling plateau above. Trend left on the increasingly indistinct path to reach the summit of Mayar, which is no more than the grassy high point of the moor in front of you (but takes longer to reach than you would think).

The continuation to Driesh is a pleasant stroll eastwards across the plateau, waymarked by a broken fence. The bealach between the two mountains lies just beyond the Shank of Drumfollow, and from it steeper slopes take you over a minor rise to the summit dome of Driesh, which is even flatter than Mayar's. To descend, retrace your steps to the Shank of Drumfollow. The Kilbo Path descends the right

Strolling across the plateau between Mayar and Driesh.

flank of the Shank, but the narrow crest of the ridge also carries a path and provides a more scenic descent as far as the forest fence at its foot, with good views left into Corrie Fee. Join the Kilbo Path at the forest fence for a delightful descent through the trees back to Glen Doll.

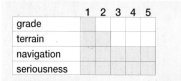

Route 42: BEN AVON • THE CAIRNGORMS

	1	2	3	4	5
grade					
terrain					
navigation					
seriousness					

OS MAP: 36
GR: 162165 (or 165176)
DISTANCE: 24 miles (39km)
ASCENT: 990m (3,250ft)
TIME: 12½ hours

Approach to Inchrory from road end
(each way):
6 miles (10km), **out** 80m (250ft)
back 30m (100ft), 2½ hr
Ascent from Inchrory:
12 miles (19km), 880m (2,900ft),
7½ hr.

ASSESSMENT: a long approach leads
to a grand plateau walk that takes in
many features of interest on one of
Scotland's most unusual mountains.
The summit tor is Grade 3.

SEASONAL NOTES: in winter the
length, remoteness and navigational
difficulty of the route make it a serious
proposition best undertaken only in
excellent conditions.

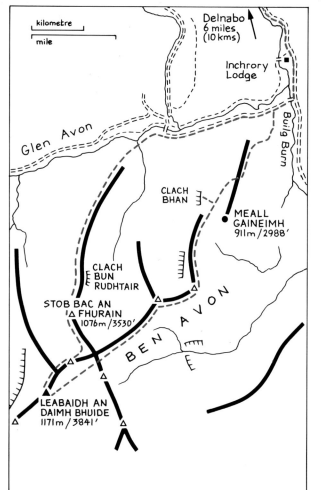

Prepare yourself for a lengthy and testing
tramp across the desolate tableland of the
eastern Cairngorms. This largest of all
Cairngorm plateaux consists of two mountain
groups, Ben Avon and Beinn a' Bhuird,
separated by the high saddle known as the
Sneck. Ben Avon is the more interesting of the
two, its slopes bristling with fascinating rock
tors rearing up to 30m (80ft) in height, and it is
best approached from the north in order to
explore the best of these.

Just reaching the foot of the mountain is an
exercise in logistics for it lies distant from any
public road; the best approach is the long walk
along the private road up beautiful Glen Avon
south-west of Tomintoul. The nearest starting
point is the end of the public road just beyond
Delnabo (GR 162165), but parking is easier a
mile back at Queen Victoria's Viewpoint car
park (GR 165176), from where a track continues to meet the private road. The road follows
the swift-flowing waters of the River Avon
through Rhine-like scenery to Inchrory Lodge.

Beyond the lodge, the now rough road
bears right into upper Glen Avon. Stay on it
until 200 metres beyond the Builg Burn, then
take a left branch up the hillside. At last
bulldozed roads are left behind (although
many can be seen scarring the hillsides) and a
path climbs the north ridge of Meall Gaineimh
to the shallow bealach between its summit and
Clach Bhan, the largest of Ben Avon's tors.
Make a short detour to explore Clach Bhan's
rocks and hollows, particularly the chair

formations, visited by pregnant women until the latter part of the 19th century in the belief that this would ensure an easy birth.

It is still a long haul to the summit of Ben Avon over several subsidiary tops, especially if diversions are made to explore the numerous interesting tors. The summit itself (Leabaidh an Diamh Bhuidhe) is the second highest tor on the mountain, set in the midst of a stony

plateau that is no place to be in mist. The tor's high point is an easy scramble from the north side. Beyond, the vast plateau continues to the flat summit of Beinn a' Bhuird, visible behind the Sneck and the huge basin of An Slochd Mor (The Great Pit), but only the most dedicated will contemplate going further.

To return to Glen Avon, descend north-east then north over Stob Bac an Fhurain and

Clach Bun Rudhtair and Stob Bac an Fhurain, Ben Avon.

continue down the north ridge past the weird fingers of Clach Bun Rudhtair, Ben Avon's highest tor. From the foot of the ridge the rough road is soon reached that leads back past the foaming Linn of Avon to Inchrory Lodge and the long walk out.

	1	2	3	4	5
grade					
terrain					
navigation					
seriousness					

OS MAP: 69
GR: 999378
DISTANCE: 8½ miles (14km)
ASCENT: 1,020m (3,350ft)
TIME: 6½ hours

ASSESSMENT: a pleasant introduction to Arran ridge walking, with the option of exploring the island's most thrilling scramble (the A' Chir ridge: Grade 5).

SEASONAL NOTES: A' Chir under snow is no place for walkers, and rather than descend from Beinn Tarsuinn to the Bealach an Fhir-bhogha it may be easier to follow the south-east ridge out towards Beinn a' Chliabhain.

The rough granite mountains of Arran provide spectacular walking. The shapely peaks, the narrow pinnacled ridges and an island setting all combine to produce exciting and addictive mountain country that is easily accessible from central Scotland. All the major peaks could be climbed in a single long day, many of them between ferries, but it is much better to savour the experience with the three routes recommended in this book (Routes 43 – 45).

The main mountain group lies north of Brodick in a rough H shape, with Glen Sannox bisecting the upper half and Glen Rosa the lower. The ridge on the west side of Glen Rosa divides into two to enclose Coire a' Bhradain, and the round of the corrie makes a good introduction to the delights of Arran ridge walking.

The route begins at the end of the road up Glen Rosa. Continue along the cart track through the farmlands of the lower glen to the Garbh Allt, then climb the left bank (right side) of this stream to a small dam. The path that climbs directly to the dam from a pipeline just before the Garbh Allt has now become dangerous and should be avoided. Above the dam, make your way across boggy ground and up the south-west ridge of Caisteal an Fhinn. On reaching the stony south top, turn right to gain the main summit. As on all Arran's ridges a good path makes the going easy.

Continuing along the ridge, an extremely pleasant stroll on moss and grass leads along the edge of the cliffs of Beinn Nuis, whose central chimney became a notorious rock climb

after an early party was forced during its ascent to attempt a human pyramid of three. Beyond Beinn Nuis the ridge continues easily to Beinn Tarsuinn, from where a contrasting steep rocky descent to the Bealach an Fhir-bhogha requires some handwork. Ahead lies the south ridge of A' Chir, the most difficult of Arran's peaks. This ridge is not included in the itinerary because it is hard and exposed, but it is the finest scramble on Arran and should on no account be missed by expert scramblers, who may even wish to explore beyond the summit to the infamous Bad Step, which all but the bravest will leave for another day.

From the Bealach an Fhir-bhogha, take the path that contours beneath the cliffs of Beinn Tarsuinn's east face to join the broad ridge leading round to Beinn a' Chliabhain. This gives spectacular views of A' Chir and Cir Mhor. The path goes over the summit of Beinn a' Chliabhain and down the south ridge towards the Garbh Allt, where the route of ascent is rejoined.

A' Chir from Beinn a' Chliabhain.

	1	2	3	4	5
grade					
terrain					
navigation					
seriousness					

OS MAP: 69
GR: 016454
DISTANCE: 8 miles (13km)
ASCENT: 1,070m (3,500ft)
TIME: 7½ hours

ASSESSMENT: an exhilarating ridge walk, with ample scrambling opportunities, superb situations and magnificent rock scenery.

SEASONAL NOTES: a major winter mountaineering expedition that is not for non-climbers.

HISTORICAL NOTE: barytes was mined commercially in Glen Sannox until the end of World War II, and miners are said to have found gold dust in the River Sannox.

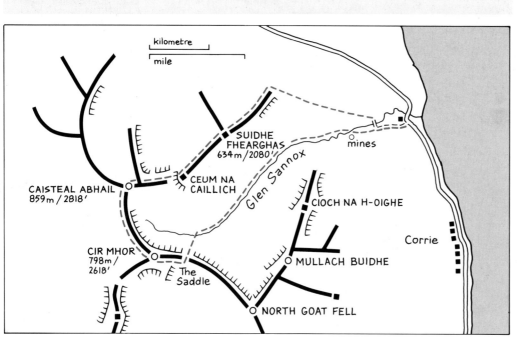

For wildness and ruggedness, few mountain prospects equal the view up Glen Sannox on Arran. The round of the sharp skyline is a magnificent but considerable undertaking, and it is perhaps best to leave the eastern peaks for another day (Route 45) in order to allow more time for the exploration of the exciting western arm of the glen.

Begin at Glen Cottage 150 metres south of the bridge over the River Sannox on the A841 and take the cart track beside the cottage up Glen Sannox. Leave the track after ten minutes, cross the river (bridge) and head across the moor to climb the rough north-east shoulder of Suidhe Fhearghas, keeping well to the right to outflank all outcrops. At the summit the rock towers that stand astride the ridge leading onwards to Caisteal Abhail burst into view, producing a shiver of anticipation.

As far as the summit platform of the first rock tower, the ridge is easy and pleasant, but take note of paths descending to the right as you will most likely need to use them to contour into the 50m (165ft) gap of the Ceum na Caillich (Witch's Step) that lies beyond. The direct descent into the gap is recommended to experienced scramblers only; it begins in a groove to the right of the summit boulder, and lower down requires an awkward thrutch down an exposed 30° slab.

From the gap, easier scrambling leads up and over a succession of rock tors to the crag-girt summit of Caisteal Abhail. The route onwards from here is barred by a line of crags that must be circumvented on the right after retracing your steps a short distance. Gentler slopes then sweep down around the head of Glen Sannox to the foot of Cir Mhor, Arran's most spectacular mountain. The ascent to its narrow summit platform is without difficulty, but the ensuing descent to the Saddle is long and steep, requiring some handwork near the top and care on loose granite granules.

Beyond the Saddle rises Goat Fell and its satellites (Route 45), but most people will have had enough excitement for one day and opt for the descent into Glen Sannox. This itself is not without interest as the steep stony path uses an eroded basalt dyke to breach a band of cliffs and gain the level confines of the glen. The path crosses the river and is boggy until the lower glen is reached, but the views of the encircling peaks compensate. Recross the river at stepping stones just before old barytes mine workings or at the bridge just beyond to rejoin the cart track back to Glen Cottage.

On the West Glen Sannox ridge.

Route 45: GOAT FELL • THE ISLANDS: ARRAN

	1	2	3	4	5
grade					
terrain					
navigation					
seriousness					

OS MAP: 69
GR: 012377
DISTANCE: 13 miles (21km)
ASCENT: 1,220m (4,000ft)
TIME: 9 hours

ASSESSMENT: an easy ascent of Arran's highest mountain followed by entertaining scrambling on narrow ridges and rock tors.

SEASONAL NOTES: in winter the ascent of Goat Fell remains straightforward as far as the upper east ridge, where steep snow may be encountered. The continuation along the north ridge to North Goat Fell and beyond may be impracticable for non-climbers.

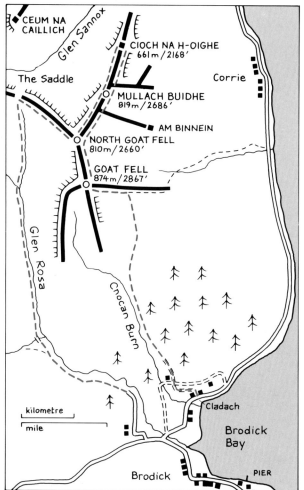

Goat Fell dominates Brodick Bay on Arran and is an obvious target for hillwalkers. Its ascent is straightforward but enlivened by tremendous seaward views and the prospect of some typically sporting Arran ridges, which await beyond the summit. The route begins as a stony track (signposted Goat Fell) that leaves the roadside opposite the hillwalkers' car park at Cladach on the north side of Brodick Bay. The track becomes a white ribbon of path that threads its way through woodland up the shallow glen of the Cnocan Burn and across moorland to the east ridge of Goat Fell. Here it joins the path from Corrie and climbs more steeply among great granite blocks, which give optional scrambling, to the summit.

The fun now begins as the route continues to North Goat Fell along the north ridge, which bristles with rock tors that can be scrambled over or bypassed on paths according to choice. The return route to Cladach goes down North Goat Fell's north-west ridge, but scramblers are recommended first to make the round trip to the end point of the north ridge at Cioch na h-Oighe (The Maiden's Breast). This adds 2 hours-plus to the day but is the best part of the route (note also that the summit of North Goat Fell can be bypassed on the way out by a traverse path).

Beyond North Goat Fell the path crosses a saddle and climbs above a buttress of sweeping slabs to the level summit of Mullach Buidhe. Broad slopes then descend to the start of a ridge that narrows excitingly between Glen

Sannox on the left and the corrie known as The Devil's Punchbowl on the right. The crest of the ridge gives some very pleasant scrambling as it leads out to the rocky summit of the Cioch, an eyrie above Sannox Bay. The return to Mullach Buidhe is just as enjoyable, as the ridge presents an entirely different challenge in the reverse direction.

The descent of North Goat Fell's north-west ridge to The Saddle is very steep and provides more scrambling. The crest of the upper section especially is more than interesting on occasion, and even the most capable of scramblers will be forced left onto an eroded path where great care is required on loose granite crystals. Continue to the cairn on the far side of The Saddle at the foot of Cir Mhor, where the path down Glen Rosa begins.

The day ends with a long but pleasant walk down the glen beside the sparkling waters of the Glenrosa Water, reaching Glen Rosa road end at GR 999378 for a 1½ miles (2½km) walk back along the road to your starting point.

North Goat Fell from Goat Fell.

	1	2	3	4	5
grade					
terrain					
navigation					
seriousness					

OS MAP: 61
GR: 544721
DISTANCE: 9½ miles (15km)
ASCENT: 1,450m (4,750ft)
TIME: 10 hours

ASSESSMENT: an exhausting, sometimes frustrating, but memorable negotiation of three famed and inimitable island mountains. A sense of humour is essential on the awkward quartzite hillsides, and the mountains are best avoided in wet weather or when shrouded in mist.

SEASONAL NOTES: unusually for Scottish mountains, the quartzite hillsides may be easier to tackle under certain snow conditions, but only the foolhardy would tackle slopes of such steepness without a rope.

The scree-girt quartzite domes of the three distinctive Paps of Jura are separated by deep cleavages, defended by miles of boggy moorland and require a determined assault, yet no mountain lover could fail to be lured to their commanding summits.

The round begins at the bridge over the Corran River just north of Lergybreck on the island's only road. Take a direct line to the head of Loch an t-Siob, aiming right of a wood and across the moor; the going is tedious but less so than beside the river. From the head of the loch climb to the bealach left of the steep summit cone of Beinn a' Chaolais and continue up steep heather among quartzite rubble. Higher up, aim for the crest of the ridge on the right to join a path that eases the final ascent to the narrow summit spine.

The route onward begins by a re-descent of the path. The going becomes very steep on awkward quartzite rocks and you are eventually channelled into a stone shoot and spewed out onto the broad bealach beneath the oppressively steep slopes of Beinn an Oir. Surprisingly, the path finds a more or less direct route up these slopes and emerges onto the right-hand skyline to follow a pleasantly tapering ridge to the summit. A causeway of stones, built by observers who manned the summit during the Second World War, continues northwards for a few hundred metres to the remains of stone huts. From here, descend right towards the bealach below Beinn Shiantaidh; steeper slopes lower down can be

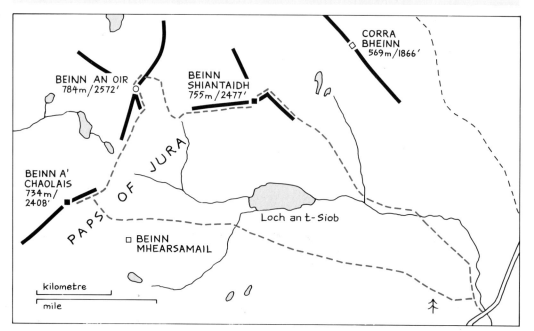

outflanked by following a grassy terrace down to the right.

The ascent of Beinn Shiantaidh is comparatively pleasant. All crags are avoided on the right and another tapering ridge leads to the summit and an extensive view over the north of the island. The descent is unfortunately nowhere near as simple. Aim for the obvious large lower cairn and then keep right, picking up an indistinct path among the rock and rubble that aims in the direction of the Corran River. You emerge on the bealach below Corra Bheinn, well to the right of all the lochans on the bealach.

The ascent of Corra Bheinn, a lower 'fourth Pap', is less severe than the three ascents so far. A path on its far side provides an easy route back to the roadside, but most walkers will have had enough by now. (The record for the Paps of Jura fell race, including Corra Bheinn, stands at just over three hours!)

Continue the descent to the Corran River and follow its left (north) bank down until it seems easier to cross to the right (south) side and take a short cut across the river's long right-angled bend directly to your starting point.

Climbing Beinn a' Chaolais, with Beinn Shiantaidh behind.

	1	2	3	4	5
grade					
terrain					
navigation					
seriousness					

OS MAP: 48
GR: 507368
DISTANCE: 6½ miles (11km)
ASCENT: 1,050m (3,450ft)
TIME: 6 hours

ASSESSMENT: after some initial hard ascent work the route develops into an enjoyable ridge scramble of Hebridean splendour and interest.

SEASONAL NOTES: the east ridge is a major undertaking under snow but rarely in condition. The route is really one to be savoured during high summer.

ROUTEFINDING NOTE: Ben More's magnetic rock makes compass work unreliable, but there are few navigational problems anyway.

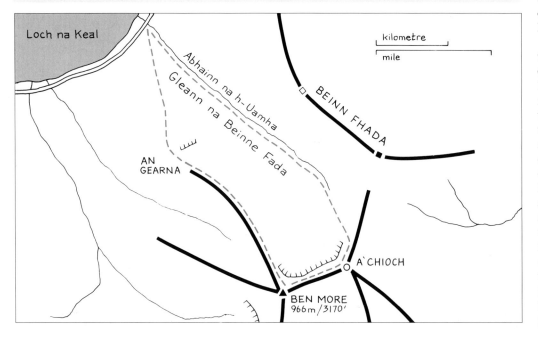

'In my journeys among the High Alps I have never found so much difficulty as here.'

The French geologist Saint Fond on attempting Ben More in 1784.

Mull is a fascinating island that has much to offer the pedestrian explorer, notably the ascent of Ben More, the only Munro in the Hebrides outside Skye. The ascent itself is unremarkable, but the views, the scramble along the connecting ridge to A' Chioch, and the descent by the picturesque Abhainn na h-Uamha make for a memorable day on the hill.

Begin on the north shore of Loch na Keal at the bridge over the Abhainn na h-Uamha, 6½ miles (11km) south of Salen on the B8035 Bunessan road. Aim directly across the gently rising but tiresome moor towards the rounded top of An Gearna, making a rising traverse to the right-hand skyline to avoid a band of crags and find better going. A large cairn at the top of the convex slope provides a welcome opportunity to pause, and then easier slopes lead to the foot of Ben More's steep, stony summit cone, whose left edge borders impressive crags. Grass runnels right of the crags ease the ascent at first, and then the best going is found at the edge itself. If motivation falters, console yourself with the knowledge that the volcano that formed Ben More was once 3,000m (10,000 ft) high and active. In any case the view, which only a Hebridean island could provide, is worth any effort.

After relaxing at the flat summit, prepare yourself for a descent of the rocky east ridge, which drops dramatically out of sight below your feet. The scrambling is easy, but fairly exposed and with lots of loose stones on ledges, which prompts most people to use as many points of contact as possible; the easiest route goes right of the crest and is well worn. Once down the steep upper part, the ridge levels off and becomes a thin wall of rock on whose crest budding tightrope walkers can practise their technique; an easy path runs below the crest on the right.

From the bealach at the end of the ridge the path climbs easier slopes to the top of the well named A' Chioch (The Breast), and then more easy scrambling is required on a series of rock steps that descend the far side. When all difficulties are past and the ridge levels out, descend the open grass slopes of Gleann na Beinne Fada all the way to your starting point. During the descent keep close to the Abhainn na h-Uamha, whose idyllic pools and waterfalls (plus a natural bridge at GR 517358) tempt one to linger on a hot summer's day.

Descending the east ridge of Ben More, with A' Chioch (The Breast) behind.

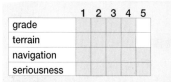

	1	2	3	4	5
grade					
terrain					
navigation					
seriousness					

OS MAP: 39
GR: 402995
DISTANCE: 12½ miles (20km)
ASCENT: 1,740m (5,700ft)
TIME: 10½ hours

ASSESSMENT: a classic Hebridean scramble with superb views; the best route in the islands outside Skye.

SEASONAL NOTES: a major winter mountaineering expedition.

ACCESS NOTE: Rum is a National Nature Reserve and authorisation for an overnight stay (hotel, self-catering or camping) must be obtained from the Reserve manager, address: The White House, Isle of Rum, by Mallaig (tel. 0687-2026). Ferries: Caledonian MacBrayne, Gourock (0687-2403), Bruce Watt Cruises, Mallaig (0687-2233), Arisaig Marine, Arisaig (0687-5224).

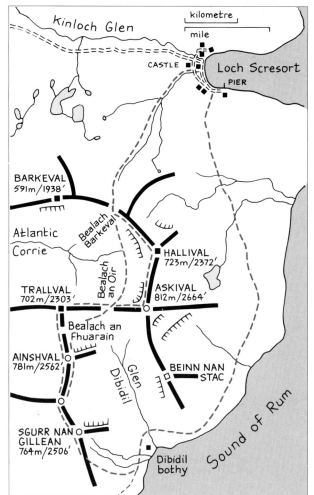

Climbing on the rugged Cuillin of Rum is an exercise in logistics and commitment, yet the traverse of the main ridge is a superb long scramble, with unforgettable views and situations on mostly excellent rock closely related to Skye gabbro. Only a brief description of the easiest line is given.

From Kinloch Castle a good path climbs beside the Allt Slugan a' Choilich into Coire Dubh, and up easy slopes to reach the main ridge at the Bealach Barkeval. Easy ground continues to the foot of the steep summit cone of Hallival, whose top is gained with minimal handwork by keeping right of crags on the ridgecrest. An easy scramble down the far side leads to a bealach at the foot of the north ridge of Askival, Rum's highest peak. From here a very narrow grassy ridge leads up to a rock tower and, behind it, the steep rock wall of the so-called Askival Pinnacle. The path bypasses the pinnacle on the left and a spot of easy scrambling gains the summit of Askival.

Keeping to the left once more to avoid the summit crags, the indistinct path now makes a long, steep descent to the Bealach an Oir and re-ascent to the east top of twin-topped Trallval. The higher west top is joined to the main ridge by a short airy side ridge that provides some of the most pleasant easy scrambling of the day. After returning to the east top, more handwork is required as the path weaves down among outcrops to the Bealach an Fhuarain, beyond which the rock becomes quartz-felsite (greasy when wet).

Ainshval rears above the bealach. The path avoids the huge buttress at its foot on slopes of grass and boulders to the right, and avoids the narrow crest of the upper ridge (which makes an enjoyable hard scramble) on easier ground to the left.

The final section of ridge is a very pleasant grassy walk from Ainshval across a dip to the subsidiary top of Sgurr nan Goibhrean and out to Sgurr nan Gillean, from where the ground drops away steeply to the sea.

It is a long way back to Kinloch by either of two routes: (1) return to the Bealach an Fhuarain, then traverse across grass slopes beneath the peaks to the Bealach an Oir and then the Bealach Barkeval, or (2) descend southwards (to avoid crags), curve down to Dibidil and follow the coast path around the eastern flank of the mountains. Both routes involve a fair amount of further ascent. The former route offers photographers evening light on the peaks and the option of climbing Barkeval for an exceptional view of the ridge, but the latter is the aesthetic way back.

The Cuillin of Rum as seen from Sgurr Dearg, Skye.

	1	2	3	4	5
grade					
terrain					
navigation					
seriousness					

OS MAP: 22
GR: 768346
DISTANCE: 10½ miles (17km)
ASCENT: 1,170m (3,850ft)
TIME: 8 hours

ASSESSMENT: a considerable but enjoyable stravaig over three isolated Outer Hebridean peaks, with scrambling opportunities on a fine high-level ridge and glorious seaward views.

SEASONAL NOTES: in winter steep snow may be encountered in several places, but the mountains are rarely in good winter condition. Beinn Mhor's summit ridge may provide some interesting, though rarely unavoidable, winter problems.

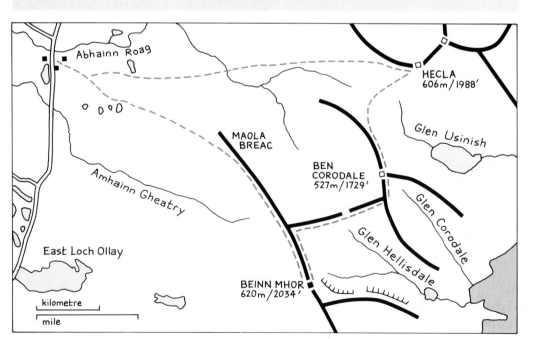

South Uist is an island with two distinct sides: its flat west coast is fringed by luxurious shell-sand beaches, while its east coast is dotted with craggy peaks rising directly out of the sea. Only Beinn Mhor breaks 2,000ft (610m), but the round of the whole Beinn Mhor group, which includes Ben Corodale and Hecla, the second and third highest hills on the island, requires twice this amount of ascent and includes a sharp ridge walk above superlative seascapes. Do not underestimate the length of the walk because of the modest height of the hills.

Begin on the A865 at the first passing place south of the bridge over the Abhainn Roag. Follow a Land Rover track up onto the moor, then make for the shoulder of Maola Breac across surprisingly dry (but surprisingly tiring) terrain. Continue up the shoulder of Beinn Mhor to reach the north-west top at the rim of Glen Hellisdale, which sports some fine 260m (850ft) cliffs containing a number of rarely tackled rock climbs. An attractive, narrow ½ mile (1km) long ridge leads onward to the main summit. It is mainly grassy, but with rocky bumps that require handwork if the crest is adhered to.

The traverse of the ridge gains from its setting, with the Sea of the Hebrides to the left and the Atlantic Ocean to the right. Islands dot the horizon all around. Far below is remote Corodale Bay, where Prince Charlie found brief respite from his pursuers before Flora MacDonald, who was born on South Uist, dressed him as her maid and aided his escape 'over the sea to Skye' in 1746, as recorded in *The Skye Boat Song*. The 'Prince's Cave' is marked on the OS map.

From the summit, return along the ridge to the north-west top. To continue the round to the summits of Ben Corodale and Hecla, two steep descents and re-ascents of about 300m (1,000ft) each are required, over grassy terrain with much exposed rock. First descend eastwards from Beinn Mhor's northern shoulder to the Bealach Hellisdale and attack the steep slope on the far side that levels off onto Ben Corodale's castellated summit, circumventing the rim of crags that guard the highest point.

Continue northwards over the summit, avoiding the summit crags once more, for the next long descent, and then gird the loins for the final ascent of the day up Hecla's steep south face. After pausing to take in the view and restore energy, descend Hecla's west ridge and tramp back across the moor to your starting point. This can be unexpectedly awkward in bad weather, because the moor is featureless and magnetic rock makes the compass unreliable, but note that all rivers flow into the Abhainn Roag.

On the summit ridge of Beinn Mhor.

	1	2	3	4	5
grade					
terrain					
navigation					
seriousness					

OS MAP: 13 or 14
GR: 183099
DISTANCE: 8½ miles (14 km)
ASCENT: 1,050m (3,450ft)
TIME: 6½ hours

ASSESSMENT: a magnificent ramble and scramble around a narrow ridge on the only Corbett in the Outer Hebrides.

SEASONAL NOTES: the steepness of Clisham's north-east face should not be underestimated when it is covered by snow. Several sections of the ridge around Glen Scaladale may also give problems in winter, although most difficulties should be avoidable.

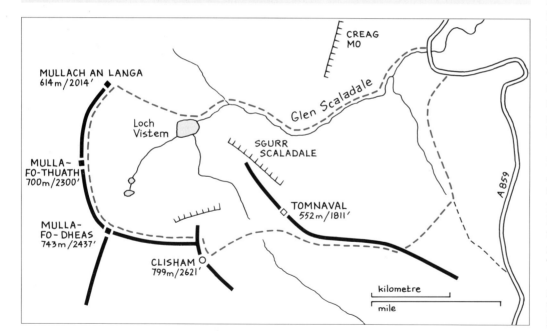

The island of Harris and Lewis is Scotland's largest island and appropriately contains the highest summit in the Outer Hebrides – Clisham. It is situated in the rugged mountain barrier that separates the rocky terrain of Harris from the peat moors of Lewis. This is rough, remote country with a distinctly un-Scottish flavour, for the landscape is barren and lonely and the hill names have a strong Norse influence.

In the long glens that penetrate the mountains there is much to explore, notably the tremendous overhangs of Strone Ulladale, the largest in Britain, and the many crags and lochans dotting the exotic-sounding mountains. Clisham, fittingly, provides the finest walking route. The traverse of the narrow ridges that connect it to its northern outliers around Glen Scaladale provide a pleasant scramble as well as a good introduction to Harris topography.

Begin at the bridge over the Scaladale River ½ mile (1km) south of Ardvourlie Castle on the A859 Tarbert – Stornaway road. Walk south along the road for 500m to pick up the obvious path crossing the hillside east of Tomnaval. Follow this path to its high point at the third of three lochans, then take to the gentle ridge rising to Tomnaval. It is best to contour left of Tomnaval's summit to avoid the 80m (250ft) descent to the saddle on the far side that separates it from Clisham. From the saddle a steep boulder-strewn ascent of Clisham's north-east face breaches a rim of broken crags at the top

and deposits you abruptly onto the narrow summit ridge.

The view is of Hebridean splendour, encompassing the whole of Harris and Lewis, Skye, the west coast of the mainland and, on a good day, the remote outpost of St. Kilda 60 miles (100km) to the west. Amid this attractive panorama the skyline of Glen Scaladale beckons invitingly. From the north-west end of Clisham's summit ridge, boulder-hop down the broad western slopes to a bealach and climb the narrow east ridge of Mulla-fo-dheas. The first half of the ascent of this ridge is on grass, then beyond a dip it becomes rocky and provides some easy scrambling.

At Mulla-fo-dheas the ridge turns northwards and descends narrowly and with interest along a cliff edge towards Mulla-fo-thuath, beyond which it broadens over awkward boulders. Continue out to the end point of Mullach

At the summit of Clisham.

an Langa for the view northwards over the vast flatlands of Lewis, then descend easy-angled slopes to Glen Scaladale. Aim for Loch Vistem and follow the Scaladale River down over rough ground between the crags of Sgurr Scaladale and Creag Mo. When a loch on the right of the river is reached a good path leads back along the left bank to your starting point.

GLOSSARY/INDEX

Note: entries are indexed by route number, not page.

111

Lyeppy an Deff *Voo*-ya, Bed of the Yellow Stag 42

Leac Mhor, Lyechk Voar, Big Slab 16

Loch a' Bhealaich, Loch a *Vyal*ich, Loch of the Pass 23

Loch a' Choire Mhoir, Loch a Chorra *Voe*-ir, Loch of the Big Corrie 37

Loch a' Gharbhrain, Loch a *Gharra*vrin, Rough Loch 36

Loch a' Mhadaidh, Loch a *Vah*ty, Loch of the Fox 34

Loch an Sgeireach, Loch an *Skair*-ach, Loch of Skerries 33

Loch an Sgoir, Loch an *Skau*-ir, Loch of the Peak 14

Loch an t-Siob, Loch an *Jee*-op, Drift Loch 46

Loch Coire Cheap, Loch Corra Chyepp, Loch of the Carp Corrie 14

Loch Fannich, Surging Loch (poss) 34

Loch Fearna, Loch Fairna, Alder Loch 19

Loch Fhionnaich, Loch Ee-*oon*ich, Cool Loch (poss) 39

Loch na Keal, Loch na *Kee*-al, Loch of (Monastic) Cells 47

Loch na Seilg, Loch na *Shell*ik, Loch of the Hunt 38

Loch nan Eilean, Loch nan *Ail*an, Loch of Islands 36

Loch Quoich, Cuckoo Loch (from Gaelic Cuaich) 19

Lochan Fada, Lochan *Fatta*, Long Lochan 33

Lochan Uaine, Lochan Oo-*an*-ya, Green Lochan 15

Long Corrie 36

Luchd Coire, Luchk Corrà, Corrie of the People (poss) or Load (poss) 37

Lurg Mhor, *Loor*ak Voar, Big Shank 25

M

Mamores, The, The Big Round Hills (literally Breasts) 11

Maoile Lunndaidh, *Mœla* Loondy, Bare Hill of the Boggy Place 26

Maol Chinn-dearg, *Mœl* Cheen *Jerr*ak, Bare Red-headed Hill 20

Maola Breac, *Mœla* Brechk, Speckled Hill 49

Mayar, Mayar, Place of Delight (poss) or Place of the Plain (poss) 41

Meall a' Chaorainn, Myowl a *Chœr*in, Hill of the Rowan Trees 11

Meall a' Chrasgaidh, Myowl a *Chrash*ky, Hill of the Crossing 34

Meall a' Mhuirich, Myowl a *Voor*ich, obscure 40

Meall Cian Dearg, Myowl Kee-an *Jerr*ak, Red Headed Hill 13

Meall Dhamh, Myowl Ghaff, Stag Hill 3

Meall Each, Myowl Ech, Horse Hill 31

Meall Gaineimh, Myowl *Gahn*y, Sandy Hill 42

Meall Garbh, Myowl *Garra*v, Rough Hill 33

Meall Gorm, Myowl *Gorr*am, Blue Hill 34

Meall Mor, Myowl Moar, Big Hill 25

Meall nan Peithirean, Myowl nan *Peh*-iran, Foresters' Hill 34

Mull 47

Mulla-fo-dheas, Mulla fo Yaiss, Summit to the South 50

Mulla-fo-thuath, Mulla fo Oo-a, Summit to the North 50

Mullach an Langa, Summit of the Heather 50

Mullach Buidhe, Mullach *Boo*-ya, Yellow Summit 45

Mullach Coire Mhic Fhearchair, Mullach Corra

Veechk *Err*achar, Summit of MacFarquhar's Corrie 33

Mullach Fraoch-choire, Mullach Frœch Chorra, Summit of the Heather Corrie 22

Mullach nan Coirean, Mullach nan Corran, Summit of the Corries 11

P/R

Paps of Jura, The 46

Princess Corrie 36

Puist Coire Ardair, Poosht Corr Ardar, Post of the High Corrie 15

Rois-Bheinn, Ross Ven, Mountain of Horses (from Norse hross) or Showers (from Gaelic Fras) 17

Rum 48

Ruadh Stac Mor, Roo-a Stachk Moar, Big Red Stack 32

S/T

Schiehallion, Shee-*hal*yon, The Fairy Hill of the Caledonians 6

Seana Bhraigh, Shenna Vri, Old Upland 37

Sgor a' Bhatain, Skorr a *Vah*tin, Boat Peak 39

Sgor a' Chleiridh, Skorr a *Chlair*y, Peak of the Cleric 39

Sgor an Iubhair, Skorr an *Yoo*-ir, Yew Peak 11

Sgor Chaonsaid, Skorr *Chœn*sitch, obscure 39

Sgor Iutharn, Skorr *Yoo*-arn, Hell Peak 14

Sgor Mhic Eacharna, Skorr Veechk *Ech*arna, MacEcharn's Peak 16

Sgor a' Chaolais, Skorr a *Chœl*ish, Peak of the Narrows 9

Sgorr Bhan, Skorr Vahn. White Peak 9

Sgorr Dhearg, Skorr *Yerr*ak, Red Peak 9

Sgorr Dhonuill (should be Dhomhnuill), Skorr *Ghon*ill, Donald's Peak 9

Sgurr a' Chaorachain, Skoor a *Chœr*achin, Peak of the Rowan Berries 24

Sgurr a' Choire Ghlais, Skoor a Chorra Ghlash, Peak of the Green Corrie 27

Sgurr an Fhir Duibhe, Skoor an Eer *Doo*-ya, Peak of the Black Men 30

Sgurr an Tuill Bhain, Skoor an *Too*-il Va-in, Peak of the White Men 31

Sgurr Ban, Skoor Bahn, White Peak 33

Sgurr Choinnich, Skoor *Choan*-yich, Bog Peak 24

Sgurr Dubh, Skoor Doo, Black Peak 31 (Slioch), 33 (The Great Wilderness)

Sgurr Fhuar-thuill, Skoor Oo-ar *Hoo*-il, Peak of the Cold Hollow 27

Sgurr Gaorsaic, Skoor *Gœr*sik, obscure 49

Sgurr Mor, Skoor Moar, Big Peak 34

Sgurr na Ba Glaise, Skoor na Bah Glasha, Peak of the Grey Cow 17

Sgurr na Bana Mhoraire, Skoor na Banna Vorar, Peak of the Lady 29

Sgurr na Conbhaire, Skoor na *Conn*avira, Peak of the Dog-men (i.e. hunters' attendants) 24

Sgurr na Fearstaig, Skoor na *Fyar*stik, Peak of the Thrift (poss) 27

Sgurr na Laocainn, Skoor na *Lœk*in, Peak of the Hero 32

Sgurr na Muice, Skoor na *Much*ka, Pig Peak 27

Sgurr na Ruaidhe, Skoor na Roo-iya, Red Peak 27

Sgurr nan Ceannaichean, Skoor nan *Kyann*ichan,

Peak of the Merchants 24

Sgurr nan Ceathreamhnan, Skoor nan *Cerr*anan, Peak of the Quarters 23

Sgurr nan Clach Geala, Skoor nan Clach *Gyall*a, Peak of the White Stones 34

Sgurr nan Each, Skoor nan Yech, Horse Peak 34

Sgurr nan Gillean, Skoor nan *Geel*-yan, Peak of the Gullies 48

Sgurr nan Goibhrean, Skoor nan *Goir*an, Peak of the She Goats

Sgurr Scaladale, Peak of the Valley of Shielings 50

Slioch, Slee-och, The Spear 31

South Uist 49

Spidean Mialach, *Speej*an *Mee*-alach, Peak of Louses 19

Srath Mhuilich, Stra *Vool*ich, Sleeve(-like) Glen (poss) 24

Srathan Buidhe, *Strah*-an *Voo*-ya, Yellow Strath 32

Sron a' Choire, Strawn a *Chorra*, Nose of Corrie 15

Sron a' Gharbh Choire Bhig, Strawn a *Garra*v Chorra Veek, Nose of the Little Rough Corrie 16

Sron Gharbh, Strawn *Gharra*v, Rough Nose 2

Sron nan Giubhas, Strawn nan *Gew*as, Nose of the Pines 8

Stob a' Choire Mheadhoin, Stop a Chorra *Mee*-an, Peak of the Middle Corrie 13

Stob an Cul Choire, Stop an *Cool* Chorra, Peak of the Back Corrie 12

Stob Bac an Fhurain, Stop Bachk an *Oor*in, Peak of the Bank of the Spring 42

Stob Ban, Stop Bahn, White Peak 11

Stob Coire an Fhir Dhuibh, Stop Corr an *Eer Ghoo*-y, Peak of the Corrie of the

Black Man 12

Stob Coire Bhuidhe, Stop Corra *Voo*-ya, Peak of the Yellow Corrie 3

Stob Coire Dheirg, Stop Corra *Yerr*ak, Peak of the Red Corrie 7

Stob Coire Easain, Stop Corr *Ess*an, Peak of the Waterfall Corrie 13

Stob Coire na Cralaig, Stop Corra na *Crab*-lik, Peak of the Corrie of the Creel 22

Stob Coire nan Cearc, Stop Corra nan *Kyairk*, Peak of the Corrie of the Hens (ie grouse) 18

Stob Coire nan Dearcag, Stop Corra nan *Jerr*-cak, Peak of the Corrie of Berries 23

Stob Coire Raineach, Stop Corra *Ren*-ach, Peak of the Corrie of Ferns 10

Stob Creag an Fhithich, Stop Craik an *Ee*-ich, Peak of the Raven's Crag 2

Stob Dubh, Stop Doo, Black Peak 10

Stob Garbh, Stop *Garra*v, Rough Peak 3

Stob Ghabhar, Stop *Ghow*er, Goat Peak 8

Stob nan Cabar, Stop nan *Kab*bar, Peak of Rafters 10

Streap Comhlaidh, Strape *Caw*ly, Climbing Adjoining 18

Streap, Strape, Climbing 18

Stuc a' Chroin, Stoochk a *Chrau*-in, Peak of Danger (poss) 4

Suidhe Fhearghas, Su-ya *Err*aghas, Fergus's Seat 44

Toll a' Choin, Tole a *Choe*-in, Hole of the Dogs 26

Tom na Sroine, Towm na *Strawn*a, Knoll of Nose 12

Tomnaval, Knoll of the Hill (from Gaelic Tom na Mheall, pron Towmna Vyowl) 50

Trallval, Giant's Mountain 48